WHO'S STROKING MY BABY?

A compelling read for anyone who has ever loved and grieved: all at the same time.

Kim Maguire

Keeper Books

Published 2016 by Keeper Books

Copyright © 2016: Kim Maguire

First Edition

A CIP catalogue record for this title is available from the British Library

This book is available from feedAread.com; Amazon.co.uk; and Amazon.com. It is also available from the author at kimmaguireruane@hotmail.com

To Lynn
I hope you
enjoy my book

love

Kim Jan 2017

For

Kieran

and Dylan

Disclaimer

I AM grateful to those of you who have been happy to be in the book. Some names have been changed where I've either been unable to contact the individual for permission to be part of my story or where the person has requested their anonymity be protected.

I'd like to stress that all of the descriptions in the book are mine and are (correctly or incorrectly) part of my memory. I'm not an historian and the details about Cyprus may not be accurate. I've tried to keep as near to the truth as possible but as the story is told from my perspective, please excuse any discrepancies you might encounter.

~ *Kim Maguire*

Contents

PART THREE

PART FOUR

#

Introduction

I STARTED to write a diary solely for me to help me work through a trauma which had occurred in my life. My diary was my therapy – I needed to relive my anguish so I could mourn my loss.

Words and tears flowed from me as I documented this life-changing event. In essence, my writing took off from the pain I began to write about. Suddenly, chapters started to evolve. But those chapters couldn't be left suspended on their own – they needed to be supported by more information. They needed propping up.

A book evolved.

In dealing with my suffering I named feelings of fear, shock, sadness, hurt, disbelief, shame, guilt and many more. I thought my feelings were unique but I soon learned they were feelings of grief. Don't others grieve too? The realisation that these emotions are universal spurred me on to write for an audience.

You are my audience. Be ready to connect to emotions you can't quite name or feelings you have suppressed. I want to look you in the eye and give that silent part of you a voice. I want to offer you the language to describe anguish.

When my mourning was complete, I was able to look back at my writing from a different point of view. I took out chapters I no longer needed – chapters of self-pity. I had come full circle. It wasn't necessary for you to feel sorry for me anymore. I was ready for you to celebrate with me.

There is hope. There is movement. Laughter will return. Connect with me and I'll bring you home.

Prologue

2009

KIERAN:

I wake suddenly. What's that? Dylan? No, he's beside me in his Moses basket.

'Kieran, Kieran!'

The same haunting shrieks.

It's my wife screaming my name.

I run into the bedroom, where less than two hours ago, I said goodnight to Kim. She was to get much needed sleep and I was to mind Dylan in the spare room.

I switch on the light. She is screeching. I soothe her.

'It's OK, you're having a nightmare. I'm here now, hush.'

'Help me! My arm has fallen off! Help me Kieran!'

She's hysterical. Her eyes are open.

'It's just a bad dream.'

She's looking at me. Something isn't right.

'I'm not dreaming. Ah my arm. Help me!'

'But Kim, your arm is fine.'

She's delirious. Has she food poisoning? We ate fish.

I manoeuvre her upright but she collapses on the bed.

'Help me Kieran! The bones are bursting through my arm. The pain!'

Her voice is ear-piercing. I lift her arm. It's heavy. I look across the landing and I see Dylan. He's still asleep. It's not making any sense. I look down at my wife who is lying across the bed. She's quiet. Hopefully she'll go back asleep. But then I hear more hollering.

'I can't feel my arm! I can't feel it!'

She's screaming even louder. She's looking straight ahead.

'Kim, look at me! Wake up!'

I am afraid. She's confused. What will I do? I don't know if this is serious but I need help. I look at the clock. Her friends are probably in bed now. I'll phone Carina, she's living nearby. One, two rings. Hurry, answer the phone.

'Hello.'

'There's something wrong with Kim.'

I try to sound calm.

'I'm coming. I'll phone Ann as well.'

Kim's blubbering. What's she trying to say?

I hear Carina on the stairs. She enters the room. We look at Kim. She is still shouting about her arm.

'What's wrong Kim?'

Kim stares blankly at Carina.

Ann might know what to do. She's on her way.

Ann appears. She tries to converse with Kim. We don't understand what Kim is saying. Ann looks at me.

'Kieran, you need to get her to hospital quickly!'

It's 1 a.m. Is it OK to phone Kim's obstetrician? He knows us. We saw him earlier today. He's a nice man. Maybe his mobile phone is turned off. I'll try him.

14

'Yes?'

Relief.

'Dr Kassinis! This is Kieran. There's something wrong with Kim. I don't know what to do.'

'Call an ambulance. I'll meet you at the hospital.'

I phone an ambulance. We've a language barrier. I don't speak Greek. I don't know the names of the myriad of roads around our rented house. What will I do?

'Kieran, take my jeep. I will stay here with Dylan.'

Ann is thinking straight.

Kim can't stand. She's mumbling. I try to reassure her.

'Everything will be fine. I promise.'

I lift Kim in my arms. It's hard to get out the bedroom door. I try again. I hear Dylan whimpering.

'Ann, he'll need feeding soon. There's expressed milk in the fridge.'

I carry her down the stairs. She's heavier than usual. Marble stairs are slippery. Don't drop her. I keep going. I'm nearly there.

I'm sweating. I see the thermometer on the wall. It's 22°C.

'Open the car door.'

I put her in the back.

Carina comes with me to the hospital. I hear Carina comforting Kim in the back of the jeep. She's holding Kim's hand.

Kim is getting sick.

'It's OK Kim. Everything will be OK.'

'I'm sorry, Carina.'

Carina is wiping Kim's face with a beach towel.

We ate fish for dinner. She might have food poisoning.

The private hospital is quiet at this time of night. The Emergency Room is closed. Carina finds a wheelchair. There are only two nurses on duty. They are unsure what to do and they want to put Kim on a ward for the night.

'No, she needs attention now!'

I look at Kim. Her eyes aren't open. She's sleeping.

'Wake up! Talk to me! Stay with me!'

She won't.

Can't they see there's something wrong?

Here's Dr Kassinis. He'll take charge. He talks to the nurses. He starts to assess the mother of my child. He looks worried. He's putting electrical monitors on my wife's chest. A nurse looks at me – I can tell it's not good. Dr Kassinis isn't engaging with me. He's preoccupied. He goes into the Nurses' Station. He won't make eye contact. A phone is handed to him. Another consultant is on his way.

Such fuss over food poisoning. She'll be fine.

The power of denial...

Part
One

Life and death

Three years earlier

2006

Kim:

THE first few weeks were the most exciting, innocent time of our lives. When my initial six-week scan confirmed there was a heartbeat inside of me, my husband, Kieran and I started telling more and more people our news, and the sheer joy on people's faces was electric. I will never regret sharing that information so fearlessly, as I would never get to do it again in such a cheery and confident manner. It was a wonderful time.

Kieran's family knew I was expecting. They too, were as excited as everybody else. My mother-in-law shared our pregnancy in a very special way and was thrilled for Kieran – he was going to fulfil his dream of becoming a father at last. She was really looking forward to her fourth grandchild being part of her family and she chatted non-stop about the great news.

She knew we were to return to Galway University Hospital five weeks later for our next scan. Kieran and I told her we'd call into her following the appointment: we'd see her within the hour.

As we sat in the waiting-room, I felt like an impostor. I was sitting in this room and I was pregnant. I had thought the

19

waiting-room was only for those trying for a baby and not for the successful.

Our nurse arrived and asked us to follow her into the examination-room for the scan.

'How are you doing?' she asked me.

'Really good and very excited!'

She gave me a look as if to say 'Be careful,' but this didn't register with me to mean anything of significance. I lay down on the bed. She lifted my jumper over my belly, turned on the ultra-sound machine, placed gel on my stomach and lifted the probe. The nurse looked at the monitor and probed my abdomen. I waited to hear how our baby was developing.

'I'm so sorry, but there's no heartbeat.' she said slowly.

'What?'

'I'm sorry.'

A terrifying sound came from the depths of my body and I let out a banshee-type cry. Kieran and I held hands and she left the room, telling us she needed to get a second opinion.

'What's going on?' Kieran asked me.

'I don't know.'

The nurse returned with a colleague but the look of sympathy on the face of the second nurse told us that this was not her first time to experience this event. She picked up the probe. My heart lightened a little.

There's been a mistake. She will find the heartbeat. She's more experienced.

But after a few minutes, she shook her head.

'I'm so sorry.'

The sound within me regurgitated.

Kieran and I held each other tightly. No one would have been able to penetrate that embrace. We needed each other like we'd never needed each other before.

The nurse sat down beside me and explained that the doctor would see me in two days' time to carry out a 'removal of the remains of a miscarriage,' and a D&C to scrape the uterine lining. I couldn't understand what she was saying, her words were beyond comprehension.

What was happening? I hadn't bled, there had been no cramps, I'd no fever or back pain. I wasn't prepared for this.

We returned to Kieran's Mum and her heart broke for us. It was her time to wail and both she and I resembled a type of macabre soprano-duet, as we bawled together in the kitchen. Kieran's silence depicted the tenor's crescendo, and on that last note we all collapsed in a heap.

The heart-breaking phone calls to my family were the audience's mute applause. Not every opera finishes the way it's expected to.

Kieran and I had been trying for a baby since we got married, nine years before. Explorative tests had been carried out but there was no apparent reason for my lack of conception. 'Unexplained infertility,' was the diagnosis. I had thought I'd fall pregnant sometime after our honeymoon. Then I thought I'd be a mother before the turn of the millennium in 2000, but as the months turned into years, the blatant reality was beginning to dawn on us. We were in that 14 per cent statistical group who would find it difficult to conceive.

There was only one thing for it.

'Will we move this year or next?' Kieran had asked me in early 2002 when we were five years married. 'We love Ballina - Killaloe so much, it might be time to become more serious about putting our Dublin house on the market and make an offer on our dream-home, the one overlooking the Shannon.'

And that's exactly what we did. We moved to the best village in Ireland and we started a spectacular life there. Socialising became a big part of our lives and friends seemed to multiply around us. The move was definitely the right decision and far exceeded our expectations – we were blissfully happy. Yet there was a void, there was still something missing. We were getting left behind when other couples were naturally morphing into families.

To optimise our chances of having a baby, we'd no choice but to go down the medical route of assisted reproduction.

The next three years of fertility treatment did not produce a baby. All of the drugs, all of the hopes, all of the excitement and subsequent devastation left us exhausted. I took endless pregnancy tests, but every time I was left disappointed.

The relentless trips to the fertility clinic had brought us closer. As a childless couple, we had spent years on our own and knew every compassionate and shadow side of each another. We were solid. We socialised with friends, went out to restaurants and encouraged each other to follow our dreams. We fought like every couple does, but soon our defences would crumble and one of us would smirk out of the corner of their mouth and normality would be restored again. We knew life without a child would be perfectly OK, but for those early years we remained steadfast in our quest for a family.

Thus, losing this baby was a bitter pill to take and returning to the clinic two days later, was always going to be tough.

Meeting Kieran

1992

DURING an interview with Gay Byrne, I heard Bono say that when he first met Ali Hewson, he knew she had a 'presence' which he didn't want to let go. I too felt that presence around Kieran when we started to date in our early twenties. I was attracted to him like no other man and was often incredulous my feelings were reciprocated.

Perhaps a descendant from the Vikings, his blond hair was his most defining characteristic. A sharp jaw-line, sallow-skin and straight white teeth all attracted my interest in him. He was from Galway and he worked as a Garda in Dublin.

Quite often people are nervous when they meet their boyfriend's parents for the first time. Not me – I met them in style. We went to Galway for the weekend to meet up with friends and we were going to stay in Kieran's family home.

I pulled the car into the driveway and Kieran and I hopped out. The rain was pounding into our faces and I had my hand up to my forehead, trying in vain to reduce the torrent of water streaming down my face smudging my mascara and causing patches of make-up to disappear.

I ran towards the light in the porch when, bang! I hit the closed glass door at full-force. Blood started to flow. I had probably broken my nose and I was somewhat dazed. Kieran, who was just behind me, saw what happened and started to laugh but when he saw my bloody nose and the gash across the top of it, he stopped. I scowled in pure disgust at his insensitivity.

Whether it was shock or mortification, my knees were buckling and my hands shaking as we entered his large modern house and ventured through the hall towards the kitchen.

'What's happened?'

'Hi Mum, this is Kim and she's just run into the porch-door.'

Could you not have thought of something else to say?

'Come in and sit down the two of you. Let me get a tissue and some ice.'

I looked around at the mahogany presses and Formica counters. The house was relatively new and the kitchen was cutting-edge for its time. Unfortunately the cream floor-tiles did little to hide the blood dripping from my nose.

'I'm so sorry.'

An oil-cloth table-covering was obscured under paper-work and half-finished mugs of coffee, and I guessed Kieran's parents had been sitting down together sorting the guest-rooms for that night in their Bed and Breakfast.

Kieran's Mum got a packet of frozen peas from her chest freezer, wrapped them in a tea towel and placed the ice-pack on my nose. Kieran's Dad was offering me vodka, which I would have loved but declined. I had wanted to make a good

25

first impression and drinking spirits as well as crying was probably not the way to go.

I can only but imagine what their conversation was when we left their house later that evening.

'What kind of girl did Kieran bring home this time? It's a pity he didn't take after our other boys and have lovely respectful girlfriends who didn't enter our house in such a melodramatic way. Ah well, I suppose it was all downhill after he got the earring and the Honda 50. We should have been stricter with him.'

We did the usual things couples do when they first date. We went for meals, to the cinema, to night-clubs and introduced one-another to our loved ones – seeking mutual approval. He got to know my family and friends and I got to know his. If one's friends are indicative of one's personality, then Kieran's friends and family validated his kind nature. He was thoughtful, he was funny, he was selfless, and he embraced life.

'I'm not going to choose one this time,' he said, walking away from the Thriller section in the local video store. 'Take a risk for once in your life. It might be a boring movie or it might be brilliant, but you have to choose it.'

He insisted I choose the movie. For me it was a challenging undertaking. In life I was afraid that I would make wrong choices. In relationships I was used to taking a back-seat and it was usually me who would massage other people's egos rather than them kneading mine. I didn't always have novel ideas and if I had, I wouldn't always voice them, lest I be ridiculed. This relationship was different from the beginning.

I took a gamble that first night and many more thereafter. It wasn't about movies, it was about respect and he respected my choices. My shy subservient ways were waning with the help of this man.

As time moved on and our relationship strengthened, we were sharing responsibilities and laughing at one another's mistakes. The laughter wasn't a cruel heckle, rather a reverent tongue-in-cheek regard for the other. He encouraged my confidence to grow and my personality to blossom, and further into our relationship I did the same for him.

UN Mission to Cyprus

2008-2009

A YEAR after my miscarriage, Kieran decided to apply for a tour of duty with the United Nations in Cyprus. Each year An Garda Síochána deployed Gardaí to assist the UN in their endeavour to maintain the status quo between the Turkish (northern) Cypriots and the Greek (southern) Cypriots. Kieran had waited eagerly to hear whether or not he'd be accepted on the mission. We had discussed the pros and cons of emigrating for a year, and it didn't take too long for us to decide that opportunities like this didn't land in our laps too often, so Kieran readily accepted his place.

Since the de-escalation of tensions between the north and south, the risk of danger to the UN staff was minimal and many Irish families were going to go as well. I took a year out of my work, which in itself was exciting. I had never taken a career-break before from teaching and this was a very new venture for both Kieran and me.

As the time approached I started to clear our house of clothes, crockery and linen and packed them into boxes to be put away into the attic. It was an exciting time – a time for change.

Kieran and some of his colleagues set off in the middle of August. I was to join him eleven days later when he was settled in. I was starting to get more nervous by the day. I wasn't sure if I was looking forward to living in another country far away from my family. I knew nothing about Cyprus and wondered how developed the country was. Pictures of ramshackle villages with no modern conveniences or social outlets, except for the odd game of backgammon in the evenings, filled my head. I was unsure if I'd be able to buy my usual cosmetics and toiletries, so I spent most of June and July sourcing a year's supply, in case I'd never see a shop again. I packed summer, autumn, winter and spring clothes, which filled large 100-litre boxes to overflowing.

'Dublin–Gatwick 11:45. Delayed: 13:10' was all that I could see on the monitor in Dublin airport.

I couldn't believe it. I wouldn't be in Gatwick in time for my connecting flight to Cyprus, and I was frantic that the first leg of my journey was going to upset all of my subsequent arrangements. Kieran was expecting me to arrive in the late evening and now our reunion dinner was scuppered.

It took me nearly eighteen long hours to get from Dublin to Cyprus and I was hugely relieved when the plane touched down and the door opened in Larnaca. I stood on the steps of the plane and felt that unfamiliar blast of heat only Northern Europeans can appreciate. It may have been 3.30 a.m., but it was hot.

Searching for my husband in the arrivals hall, I heard the distinct sound of a voice I recognised.

'Kim, over here.'

As I heard him call my name, I looked around and was speechless. Kieran's hair was blonder than when I'd last seen him and he had a healthy look from the Mediterranean sun. He was wearing a UN uniform, and looked more handsome than I'd remembered. The less formal UN attire, aesthetically superior to the one he wore in Ireland, was also more flattering. Gardaí at home could take a leaf out of the UN book, and could actually look smarter if they swapped their wool trousers for navy cotton combats, exchanged their blue Garda shirts for white crisp polo shirts and got rid of the official-issue clip-on tie. An instant makeover transformation could occur. (I thought about writing a letter to Commissioner Murphy with this suggestion but reckoned he might have other pressing issues to deal with.)

'You look great!' I said, embracing him for the first time in nearly two weeks.

'Hi, so do you,' he lied, as he kissed my two tired pink cheeks, and then quickly withdrew from me after getting a whiff of my stale breath.

I'm working in four hours' time, so come on, let's get going.'

I followed him to the exit.

I sensed the stress in his voice and looking at his slouched shoulders, I think I was more pleased than he was to reunite.

In case I hadn't heard the first time, he repeated, 'It's nearly 4 a.m., I've to go to bed, get up at seven and then drive an hour to work in the United Nations Protected Area (UNPA) in Nicosia.'

Kieran was never a man to survive too well on a lack of sleep, so collecting me early in the morning didn't enhance our big reunion. I was also exhausted after my long day, so we put off our catch-up chat until the next day. Sleep was a priority.

Half of the Irish Contingent group of eighteen was only just settling into their new jobs and Kieran hadn't yet found a house for us to live in. One of the Irish Gardaí, John, had kindly offered us a bedroom in the basement of his house until we got sorted, and as we arrived to his house in the dawn, all I could make out was dust, heavy machinery and what amounted to a building site. I wondered what I'd got myself into. I'd been right all along, I had arrived in an uncivilised country.

The heat was stifling when I got up a few hours after Kieran's departure to work. I love hot temperatures but I'd never experienced such humidity before. When I opened the front door I was blasted with the smell of dead heat, there was a lack of oxygen in the air and I found it hard to breathe.

I stepped out of the door into the carport, wiped the sweat off my brow, and assessed the landscape around me. Amazing blue skies, freshly planted palm-trees, gleaming tiles and new concrete surrounded the house. There was a rectangular-shaped swimming pool in the garden, and the building-work which I had noticed the night before was actually left-over bricks from a recently built garden wall.

It was eerily quiet in the new complex of apartments and four-bedroomed houses, and I guessed the other tenants were either working or still in bed.

I ventured out to one of the sunbeds with my beach towel, sun cream and a bottle of water. I lay down for five minutes but I was too hot. I tried to sit up and could see beads of sweat glistening in the sun on my body. The perspiration flowed between my breasts, lodged in the skin crevasses just above my stomach, before trickling down either side of my abdomen.

Jesus! I'm roasting. I need to cool down now.

The soles of my feet scorched as I made the five-foot trip to the poolside. I slithered into the fresh cool water, swam a little and climbed up onto an air-mattress which was bobbing up and down in the middle of this haven. It was beautiful here. My thinking was changing. Perhaps I had been mistaken. This country was going to have a lot to offer and southern (Greek) Cyprus was very much a first world country.

The sound of distinctive Irish male voices was getting closer. There was a discussion about a Wexford hurling game of some sort, goals, points, off-side etc. Growing up in the rugby scenes in South County Dublin had ill-equipped me with any knowledge of the GAA, other than remembering it was founded in 1884. I knew that if the men were coming my way, I'd have to feign interest. No problem: I was quite an expert. What wasn't going to be so easy was exiting the pool elegantly.

The voices were only metres away. I had to act soon but I was too late – I'd an audience. I had no choice but to self-consciously clamber out of the pool, at the same time I incompetently straightened my bikini top and wiped water away, which was threatening to drip from my nose.

The two men were obviously part of the Irish Garda Contingent and as they approached me, one of them extended his hand.

'Howya. I'm John. You're very welcome.'

Living in Ireland, it's more than unusual to meet your husband's work colleagues wearing your bikini. I didn't know what the proper etiquette was, and I'm sure it wouldn't be found in any of An Garda Síochána Rules and Regulations' handbooks. Did I pop my boob back into its rightful place or did I shake hands first? Perhaps my indecency issue needed to be tackled first and as their gold wedding-bands caught the sun's reflection, I knew their wives would have thought my decision a smart one.

When the niceties were over and introductions complete, John said, 'Come on, I'll show you some of the island; it's too hot here.'

I nodded in agreement.

'I'm not working until later today so I've plenty of time to show you where I'm working in Pyla.'

'That would be great.'

I was burning up in the sun and as I'd just arrived and had no car; I'd nowhere else to go.

'I have a UN jeep here, and although there's no air conditioning, it should be much cooler than outside.'

This sounds interesting.

Introduction to the island

WE were living in the Pyla tourist area just outside Larnaca. It was an unusual place. Some houses were only half built and there were plenty of empty undeveloped sites. In contrast to the unfinished buildings, bespoke houses stood behind wrought iron gates and luscious greenery fell out over the garden-walls onto precariously-built footpaths. The beautifully manicured gardens were watered by sprinklers, an extravagance which I'm sure was adding to the water shortages on the island, and reminding me of the article I had read on the plane about the urgent importation of water tankers from Greece.

The tourist trade was big in this area and a lot of the houses were built as summer homes. Tourists liked to have swimming pools in their gardens but Cypriots had no need for a pool. Instead of lying outside on sun-loungers, they went to work and stayed indoors with the air-conditioning on. Sunshine is not a novelty for those who experience it most days of the year.

Many of the houses were worth more than half-a-million euros, some were Cypriot owned and others were bought by Europeans and Russians. Cyprus had been ruled by the United Kingdom from the end of the nineteenth century until 1960 and there was still a strong British influence on the island. Cypriots drove on the left-hand side of the road and a lot of Cypriots were bilingual, speaking both Greek and English.

The terrain began to change as we drove towards Pyla village. There were no more footpaths, just dry-scorched fields with little sign of tourist activity.

'Here we are,' John said. 'It's a bit different, isn't it?'

The village was the antithesis of the beachside-resort I'd just seen and was exactly what my imagined impression of Cyprus had been. It was small and typical of Mediterranean villages of long ago. Looking dull and nondescript in the now clouded sky, the buildings were uninviting and not to my taste. Cars were covered in dust particles blown in from arid fields surrounding the small village.

John showed me the UN police station where he and other international members of UN contingents were working. It was overlooked by a Turkish Army lookout-tower which was on a cliff imposing on the village with its intimidating height. Pyla was the only bi-communal village in the Buffer Zone where half of its inhabitants were Greek Cypriots and the other half Turkish Cypriots. The complexity of the Cypriot Problem had gone on for hundreds of years and the island had a long history of tension.

A smell of spices was in the air, and I'd to lift my hand to cover my nose from the strong scent. It was a peculiar place and held a different energy for me. I looked around to see why I felt uncomfortable. Was it the silence or an underlying tension? The two communities sat in different cafés drinking coffee, rarely engaging with others from the opposing side. There was no wealth to be seen here, just ordinary local people getting on with their daily lives, unaffected by the affluence I had observed where we were staying a few kilometres away but very affected by the 'Cypriot Problem'.

'Do you think Kieran will be finished work yet?' I asked when we got back into the jeep.

'We'll go, have some lunch and by the late afternoon he should be finished.'

By the time Kieran returned I was back at the pool chatting to some of the other Gardaí who had also rented apartments in the complex. They had finished work and because I had got over my previous modesty issues, relaxing by the pool with a glass of wine wasn't so bad after all. The heat was less intense and it was very pleasant lying in the warmth of the evening sun.

'I see you're fitting in well.'

I turned around and saw Kieran. He was in the same UN uniform I'd seen him wear many hours before. However, the crispness of his polo shirt had disappeared and sweat now stained and dampened it. His combat-trousers and black boots were covered in dust and he looked as though he needed a beer.

'It's not so bad I suppose. The guys have been very accommodating.'

'I'm just going to change first,' he said, 'and then go for a swim.'

When he was ready I got into the water with him.

'Tell me everything that's happened since you arrived here.' What's it like?' I asked.

'So far so good.'

'What's work like?'

'I'm only settling in.'

'If you're being coy, then I'm going to fill you in on my news. I was up in Pyla village with John this morning. It's all very interesting but I'll probably never understand the history of the country and am sure to embarrass you when I embellish information I know little of.'

'It's a sensitive issue with the Cypriots. Be careful what you say to people. You just don't know what's happened to them and their families in the last thirty years.'

I blabbered on for a while and only then noticed the poolside area was empty.

'Come on, let's go and meet the guys in Andy's Bar,' Kieran said, a bit too eagerly for my liking.

I had thought we'd go out on our own.

'Whatever,' I replied annoyed.

Our reunion was less intimate than I'd anticipated but I knew Kieran well and could see he was keen to get to know the others. I tried not to look too dejected and when we were ready, we walked hand-in-hand to the pub.

Andy's Bar was owned by a small Greek Cypriot, Andy, who was in his fifties. He mumbled and smiled when he collected glasses and took orders. The bar had fridges which were jam-packed with bottled beer and soft drinks. There were bottles of gin, whiskey, vodka, Bacardi and other spirits resting on the counter behind the bar. The ceiling was decorated with Irish county-jerseys and Guinness signs. Andy had a small popcorn machine and he would hand out free salted popcorn to entice customers to stay in the pub after 10 p.m. – not that Irish punters needed too much encouragement.

This was the Irish hangout and we had great fun here. In the summer we sat outside on small aluminium chairs and wobbly tables, and in the winter we would sit inside on the same cold chairs. There was a calendar with pictures of page-three models, two outdoor pool tables and a large television showing Premier League soccer matches. Some would have been appalled by this meagre pub with worn carpet tiles, a jukebox and a spiral staircase which brought you to a very modest toilet but the muted décor was in stark contrast to the vociferous ambiance.

Nonetheless, it was our hostelry and in the evenings belly-laughter was always guaranteed.

Three Irish families who had finished their year in Cyprus were celebrating their final night in the bar. They were making way for the new Irish Contingent to take over from them, and were advising us on sites and resorts to visit on the island.

'You have to go to Pissouri. It's amazing. Paphos has a lot to offer too. Definitely go up north to Kyrenia and the Karpas Peninsula. They're a must. When you cross the border into Northern Cyprus you can buy imitation designer goods like Gucci and Mulberry handbags,' one of the enthusiastic wives told me.

Me buy imitation designer-bags? I don't think so! I only do the real thing.

'When the men are working, there's plenty for you to do. Make sure you meet up for breakfasts, lunches and barbeques with the other girls. This will be the best time of your life – make the most of it.'

An exciting new life was beginning.

Meeting the wives

ON THE second morning of my new life, I was invited for breakfast by the wife of the Irish Contingent leader. The Irish families who were already living in Cyprus were very good to the newcomers and the women had arranged the breakfast to welcome the new wives and children who had just arrived. This was a kind gesture and I was appreciative of it.

My clothes dilemma started from the night before. I didn't know what to wear and changed my outfit three times until I was eventually ready.

I know there's a swimming-pool in the garden but will we be indoors or outdoors; in the pool or not? Feck it! I'll put on my bikini under a white vest top and denim mini. I hope I'll look OK.

As I nervously entered the house, one of the girls came over to me and said, 'Hi, you must be Kim, come in.'

What are they wearing?

Phew! They're dressed similar to me.

I felt at ease straight away. We sat in the kitchen with fans on at full speed. The temperature was in the high 30s. It was a newly built house and was situated in the middle of the tourist area in Pyla (three minutes from Andy's Bar.) We ate rashers and sausages, drank copious cups of tea and chatted as only a group of women can.

I was sitting next to one of the women, Sinéad, who had arrived to Cyprus the previous week. She was a few years younger than me and had striking dark hair which contrasted beautifully with her pale skin.

'I've taken a year's career-break from teaching,' I said. 'I hope I've done the right thing.'

'I've actually resigned from my job,' she replied, 'so I'm really hoping the year will be worth the huge sacrifice I've made.'

'Yes hopefully. I hear some of the families are meeting up in Agia Napa Waterpark next week. Are you going to go?'

'Absolutely, I might even text some of my ex-work colleagues from beside one of the waterslides.'

'They'll kill you!'

Our friendship started from that moment and we developed what was going to be a very strong link. Friendships were what this trip was about. The weather was fantastic, the lifestyle was brilliant but what it boiled down to was the people.

After breakfast Sinéad and I were shown around some of the surrounding villages of Pyla and we went into the nearest city, Larnaca. This wasn't an historical or geographical tour but rather a shopping trip, which at that time was perhaps of more relevance to me than what I had seen the previous day in Pyla village. We went to the large international supermarket, as well as Debenhams, Zara, Dorothy Perkins, Marks & Spencer and many other high-street stores.

My kind of expedition.

Over the following weeks the rest of the female partners arrived with their children and the serious task of socialising

41

started. Babysitters were found and we'd meet up in Andy's most nights for chilled bottled beers, ouzos and G&Ts. It was a fresh start for everyone. We all had our own reasons for leaving our Irish lives behind for a year and were very happy living protected lives far away from the weakening Celtic Tiger.

I also became friendly with Carina who lived quite close to me in Pyla. Carina was smaller than me and had blond highlights in her hair. She had three young children who kept her busy and whom she adored. Her sense of humour was infectious and her smile lit up her face enhancing her blue eyes. At times I was envious of her outgoing personality and when we were in Andy's, she was able to laugh and joke with everyone.

The ultimate Irish mammy, she was more hospitable than anyone I had ever met. Electricity bills didn't bother her. The kettle in her kitchen was constantly switched on and the 'Mrs Doyle' in her commenced.

'You'll have a cup of tea,' she said one day I was visiting.

'No thanks.'

'Go on, you will.'

'No, I'm too hot.'

'Ah, go on. I'm having a cup.'

'OK then,' I conceded.

'Why don't you go outside and I'll bring it out with some biscuits?'

An umbrella shaded the patio-table and I pulled out one of the six chairs, sat down with my phone and started to read a text from Mum.

'Look I got a new tractor.' one of her boys said, running up to me.

'Lucky you, it's fabulous!' I said to him, examining it and casting my phone aside.

His twin brother approached with a similar vehicle and they began to argue over who owned which.

All of a sudden Carina appeared through the French doors.

'Boys, stop throwing your toys. Go and spray each other with the hose in the garden. Leave us alone for two minutes. No. Stop. Use the toilet!'

'Oh dear. Too late!' I said. 'Never mind. Did I tell you my parents have booked their flights and are coming over for a fortnight?'

'Yes you did, many times. You keep talking about them going to the function in the Ambassador's next month. My parents would love to go too, but they've only just gone back to Ireland.'

Our visits to one another's houses were daily. I always enjoyed Carina's company and we'd chat over cups of tea in the sweltering heat. What else would non-working women do?

'I've found a house for us,' Kieran said later that day when he got home from work, 'let's go and take a look.'

The house was half a kilometre from the beach and close to some of the other Irish UN families. It was four years old and the floors were tiled throughout. Upstairs, there were two double bedrooms of equal size. The typically designed tourist-house had two bathrooms, cream leather sofas and a modern

43

kitchen. There were three sets of patio-doors which we kept open to generate a breeze throughout the house.

A rectangular shaped pool was overlooked by a yellow slide at the far end of it. A gardener came twice a week to service the pool and cut back the shrubs and lemon trees which were in surrounding borders. Sprinklers kept the grass growing and the gardener ensured this garden stayed alive – had it been up to me, the garden would have resembled a cemetery within a week. The only shaded area outside the house was in the carport, where I would have to hang out the washing to protect the clothes from the intense sun which bleached their colours.

After moving in, our mammoth boxes arrived from Ireland full of clothing, kitchen utensils, bedding and toiletries, and as I looked at the numerous bottles of shampoos, sun creams, antiperspirants, mosquito repellents, plasters, tea towels, saucepans and much more, I realised I should have done some research into the economy of the island and learned that all of these products were for sale in Cyprus too.

'Oh my God, I'm so embarrassed! We brought so much stuff over. I'm sure we won't use half of it.' I said to Carina.

'You think you're bad, we've about double that amount. I've my Christmas presents for the kids bought and wrapped.'

Between us, we probably had enough to set up a corner shop.

Joyful news in Pissouri

THE women accompanied their spouses on this yearlong UN mission to Cyprus. We were the self-named WAGs and were sometimes to be seen in packs. We had the luxury of knowing we'd only be spending the year together, so it was quite acceptable to live out of each other's pockets.

A few months into the year we decided it was time to go on a pampering night away.

This time I'd done my research before I left. I knew we were going somewhere very special, to a secluded beach-resort in Pissouri Bay situated between Paphos and Limassol in the south of Cyprus.

The old village of Pissouri was on one of the hills two kilometres from the hotel. The village was beautiful; sparsely populated with cute-characteristic taverns, shops and magnificent panoramic views. Further down the valley, stunning white cliffs rolled as far as a pebbled beach and turquoise sea in the Bay of Pissouri. The hotel was situated in the bay and was surrounded by vineyards and orchards. I fell in love with it all before I'd even stepped out of the car.

We travelled in convoy, three women per car. When we checked into the hotel and sorted out our sleeping arrangements, we were brought by a porter in a buggy to our bedrooms which were in two-storey chalets outside. Pathways connected the hotel's bedrooms to the main building and were wide enough for the baggage-loaded buggy to meander through. Luscious palm trees, shrubbery and green grass were an integral part of the well-manicured gardens. It was an exclusive hotel for well-heeled clientele.

On this overcast November day, the views out onto the outdoor restaurant, infinity pool and the beach were slightly marred. The winter was slowly approaching and the afternoon temperatures were beginning to drop. I went into the spa and lounged on a bed by the edge of the indoor pool. No uncomfortable, sun-loungers were to be seen in here – only cream-covered mattresses on beds dressed with blue plumped up cushions.

An employee of the hotel approached me and attempted to create a conversation.

'How long you are staying in Cyprus? Do you like the hotel?' I think she might have asked, but my mind was consumed by other things.

Could I be pregnant?

Even though I had brought a pregnancy test with me, I kept telling myself not to be so foolish and to stop torturing myself with such far-fetched notions.

That night when I was getting ready for bed I went into the bathroom. The tiled floor was cold under my bare feet and I slipped on a pair of white hotel slippers, indulging in the luxury the hotel afforded its guests. I reached into my wash-bag and taking a pregnancy test out of a side pocket, I opened the box, took out the test stick and vigilantly hid it from my roommate on a shelf above the bath. I wanted to be as quiet as

I could so as not to create any suspicion when I got up the next morning.

The television displayed the time. It was midnight. The white crisp sheets engulfed my body and I snuggled into the large single bed and drifted into a restless sleep. The countdown started: 3 a.m., 5 a.m. Eventually it was 6 a.m. I couldn't suspend my trip to the bathroom any longer.

I tiptoed in, took down the pregnancy stick and did what I was an expert at doing. Another countdown: 30 seconds, 60 seconds, and then two minutes. It was time. I slowly turned the stick over, anticipating the worst. I studied the blue lines in the windows. Two were clearly visible.

I was pregnant!

I crept back into bed and lay stunned under the bed clothes. Kieran was in Manchester on a stag weekend and wasn't due back until later that evening. My heart was thumping. I had to tell him but it was still very early in the UK and even though I was ecstatic, I knew he'd a long day of travel ahead and would need to sleep some more.

I got up and went for breakfast to absorb the enormity of the moment. Presuming I wouldn't meet anyone this early, and wanting some time alone, I waited to be shown to a table. But one of our group, Sinéad, had gone for an early-morning walk, was bright and cheery and was already eating a bowl of granola in the dining-room. She motioned for me to sit with her. I approached smiling and pulled out the chair opposite her.

'Good morning.'

'Hiya, how did you sleep?'

No sleepless night for her.

'Great thanks. Go on up to the buffet and help yourself,' she coaxed.

My head was buzzing but I wasn't in form for breakfast. Nonetheless, mirroring what most Irish people do at a free-for-all buffet, I greedily piled my plate with rashers, sausages, toast and freshly baked croissants. The smell of the cooked breakfast wasn't as appealing as it normally was and when I returned to my seat I started to pick at the food on my plate.

'Did you enjoy the party in the Ambassador's residence last weekend?' Sinéad asked.

'Wasn't it brilliant?'

'Did you see the Persian rugs on the parquet floors and the photos of various dignitaries with the Ambassador?'

'Sorry, what did you say?'

I wasn't concentrating.

Oh my God, I'm pregnant!

'You know what I mean – the views and the opulence. I've never been to that suburb of Nicosia before. I didn't even know there were private swimming pools in the capital city. Didn't the kids have such a ball jumping in and out of the pool?'

'Yes, it's amazing to be invited to such posh afternoon parties. My parents loved it too. I suppose it's just another perk of accompanying our men on the UN mission!'

Shit! I can't believe I'm pregnant!

I felt bad cutting our conversation short but I had to leave in search for some solitude. I needed to think – to get away from the hotel and get some air.

A tiny ornate chapel was hidden away in a stone building to the left of the garden path overlooking the sea. I crept silently through the door, past the eight wooden chairs and studied the magnificently decorated walls. I prayed in the silence at the oratory.

Please God let this be true. Don't trick me. Don't take it from me.

I wandered around aimlessly before walking down some steep steps towards a long stone path which was bringing me away from the hotel. I had to ensure I'd have privacy for the most important phone call I was going to make.

All I could hear were the waves crashing against the stony shore and I hoped their thunderous noise would not disrupt my phone conversation. Three tourists were out walking in the distance. I turned away and put my hand into my jeans' pocket and took out my phone. My fingers shook as I tapped the pre-fixed number and dialled Kieran's phone.

For the second time in my life I was going to say these three words. Kieran answered the phone on the third ring.

'Hiya,' he said sleepily. 'Are you OK?'

He had been out the night before and I knew it might take him a few moments to wake up. I didn't say anything for about five seconds, pretending there was some kind of time delay between the two countries. I wanted to give him time to open his eyes and orientate himself. I needed him to take in what I was going to say. I braced myself.

'Kieran I've some news.'

'What news?'

'I am pregnant!' How I loved saying those words. 'I've just done a pregnancy test and I'm pregnant.'

I waited for a reaction of some kind. There was only silence and some nasal sounds which I couldn't identify.

'I'll phone you back,' he mumbled.

I could barely hear his voice and I wondered if the background sound of the sea was causing static between us. I stood there frozen.

Was he disappointed with the news? Why did he hang up?

I held my phone and looked at the screen in shock. I was supposed to be savouring this moment, the way I had when I had told him I was expecting two years ago when we had hugged one another for ages. Now I didn't know what to think.

The Nokia ring-tone made me jump and I answered feeling confused.

'Kim, this is unreal. Are you sure? I had to hang up. I couldn't stop crying. Tell me what happened. Tell me everything.'

I revealed the happenings of the morning as clearly as I could, but he couldn't understand a word I was saying. There was just too much to take in.

Going to Cyprus had been a very good move. Lying on the black-coloured sand on Pyla beach for three months had paid off. Long walks along the seashore, kicking the foam of white rolling-waves, were obviously what my body was craving. Swimming for hours in the warm Mediterranean Sea had been imperative for relaxation but most of all, it was happiness. That had been the key. I was the happiest I'd ever been. I was confident in myself, my body self-image was at an all-time high and I was living an ideal life. These months of spectacular living were the best months of my life and finding out I was pregnant was now the icing on the cake.

Nothing could go wrong.

Nearly losing something precious

THE week leading up to my first scan caused me many sleepless nights. I had been saving the pregnancy news for three months and the second Friday in the middle of January was going to be the time to tell my family and friends in Ireland that I was pregnant. Each time I had spoken to Mum on the phone during those early months, I'd been filled with many powerful emotions. I'd been dying to tell her I was expecting but I had kept the secret safe without mentioning a word. Only one month into the pregnancy my speech was practised in my head: 'I've wonderful news. You're going to be a granny again. I'm three months pregnant!' I'd pause and let her 'oh 'and 'ah' before continuing, 'I've had my scan and I could see little fingers and toes and everything is going really well so far.'

I couldn't wait for the scan to be over so I could make my phone calls.

Kieran and I decided to go out for dinner the night before the scan.

'I can't believe it. We've only fourteen hours to go. I can't wait to break the news. I'm so excited!'

Kieran leaned across the restaurant table and put his hand out to touch my fingers. We smiled at each other.

'Yes, it's mind-blowing. My Mum will be thrilled too.'

The small restaurant in Pyla was heaving, as though our neighbours were all out celebrating with us. Waitresses were flitting from table to table but the service was slow. The strong smell of burning steak and the noise of an arguing couple, did little to dampen our spirits. Our dinner arrived and was placed in front of us, without a smile or a word from the waitress.

'What a miserable girl,' Kieran said.

'Who cares? Tonight's a night to remember. Look around. Take it in. This is the last time we'll be in public protecting our secret.'

'I love you so much.'

'You too,' I echoed.

I took a long sip of my ice-cold Sprite and started to eat.

Suddenly, I felt a rush of something.

I ran to the Ladies.

Blood was pouring out of me.

Kieran broke every amber light to get us to the maternity hospital. My eyes remained dry. I wasn't upset. I was in shock.

Larnaca was quiet at this time of the night. Commuters had already returned home. Neon lights flashed at no one in particular and an eerie calmness helped me to concentrate on my breathing – in and out in a controlled manner.

It was our first time to visit this hospital. We got out of the car and ran towards the main entrance. We stepped into the foyer and looked around.

The hospital was modern with freshly-painted walls. Some patients sat quietly outside consultation-rooms waiting to be seen by their doctors. I looked at a sign explaining doctors' clinics were open all evening until 8 p.m. A clock on the wall showed it was now 8:05 p.m.

We approached a desk where an exhausted-looking receptionist lifted her head from behind her computer.

'Kalispera,' she said yawning, embarrassingly putting her hand up to her mouth.

'Kalispera, hello, my wife is pregnant and is bleeding and we need to see a doctor.'

She jumped up from behind her computer.

'Dr Kassinis is still here and he might see you.'

The now animated receptionist walked across the corridor, knocked on a door and spoke to the doctor in Greek. She then turned to look at me and said, 'Come to this room.'

We entered the room where a doctor was sitting at a desk.

'Hello. Sit down please. Tell me what is wrong.'

Dr Kassinis was unperturbed as he wrote down my details. He was a sallow-skinned man in his fifties and had dark hair which was showing early signs of aging. His eyebrows were dark and he had a friendly round chubby face which put me at ease, that is, until his demeanour changed when he started to scan the baby in my uterus.

There was urgency in his voice and he looked me in the eye.

'The placenta is come from uterine wall. Look here at scan.'

I looked but all I could see was our tiny little baby for the first time.

'Is it serious?' I asked.

'Very, very serious. You staying in hospital tonight and not going from bed. I will know better tomorrow.'

His broken English was fluent to us. We understood every word he was saying and our faces dropped once more.

We knew the drill.

We'd been at this stage before and were resigned for the worst.

The bleeding still hadn't stopped and I was put in a wheelchair to go upstairs to a hospital bed. I had to lie horizontally in the bed for the night and a nurse hooked me up to an IV drip to stop the bleed. Kieran looked at me and I at him as the nurse took a blood sample from my arm. Her sympathetic demeanour was more evident when she handed me an electronic bell to press during the night to alert the staff, when everything kicked off, so to speak.

I knew things weren't good and I knew what she was thinking.

There was a hint of a smell of disinfectant in the air. The staff obviously took great care, time and pride in their work. The hospital was spotless: no infectious diseases were going to penetrate the germ-free walls.

This was a private hospital and each maternity room had two beds, one for the female patient and the other for her partner. The room was large and resembled a warm hotel bedroom. Pressed-white sheets covered the beds and the blue blankets resting on the sheets had dry cleaning tickets stapled in the bottom right-hand corner of them. A flat-screen TV with a computer keyboard and a *Playstation* (perhaps to be used by the expectant Dad waiting for his partner's onset of labour) were on a shelf facing the twin beds.

Except we weren't in this room preparing to give birth or to watch the 28 inch TV screen. I was here trying to hold onto the little life within me. I wasn't examining the nice toiletries, and the not-so-plush extra-large sanitary pads which were resting on a shelf over the wash-hand basin in the ensuite bathroom.

The rooms may have been comfortable but aesthetics don't always mirror the reality that goes on within them.

At the end of the day a hospital is a hospital.

Kieran stayed the night with me. Every hour was agonising and we couldn't sleep, somehow thinking that by staying awake would prevent a miscarriage. I cried all night long with only short periods of quiet exhaustion when no tears fell. My heart was crumbling.

'How are you doing?' Kieran asked all through the night and then would answer his own question. 'I'm terrified. Is this it? Is this the end of the road for us?'

'I'm going to pray to every person I know who might help to keep our baby alive.'

'This can't happen to us again. We've been trying for a baby for eleven years. Why us?'

Why us, indeed?

The light outside was turning from artificial street-lighting to a natural light and I looked at the clock on the wall. It was 6 a.m. and I could breathe again. I had survived the night and I hadn't pressed the bell once. The baby had remained inside me.

Dr Kassinis entered the room carrying a portable ultrasound machine.

'How are thing? The nurse said no bleeding anymore.'

'No, it stopped a few hours ago.'

He made no reply.

He took out the probe, put gel on my abdomen and started to look for life. I closed my eyes and waited for those agonising words; 'There's no heartbeat.'

'All good. No sitting up or leaving the bed. You must lie flat for three days.'

'The baby is still alive.' I said, hugely relieved.

Our little baby was strong and had no intention of ending his precious little life. Dr Kassinis sensed my mood.

'It's serious! You must do all I say. The placenta is not attaching proper yet.'

I was at his mercy and was obedient in all I did – it was the least I could do for the baby. If he was hanging on by a thread, I had to offer him the best chance possible.

When we were on our own again I said to Kieran, 'What happens if Mum finds out I'm here? I'll have to phone her today. What do you think?'

'Yes we should.'

I had only been hours away from exploding with the great news but now I was sombre when I dialled my parents' landline.

Dad answered the phone.

'Hi Dad. It's Kim. Is Mum there?'

'Oh Kim. Hi. How are you?'

'Fine. Can you get Mum?'

'I think she's in the shower. I'll wait 'til she's finished. It's lashing here and really wintery. The cattle are frozen in the fields and I'm up to my eyes. What's the weather like in Cyprus?'

'Dad I'm pregnant. Get Mum.'

'She's coming.' He barely had time to say the words, panicky, handing the phone to her.

'Hi love, are you OK?'

'Are you sitting down?'

'Go on, I'm just out of the shower and am dripping water all over the carpet.'

'I'm pregnant.'

'What? Let me sit down.'

Envisaging her trembling on the bed with her wet hair tossed messily on her head, I told her what I had planned to tell her for all of those months. She listened without interruption, only the odd 'Oh my God' coming from her mouth, and I could hear her concern when she was assimilating all I was saying.

She was reluctant to hang up, hoping her kind words could ensure I'd have a safe pregnancy.

From then on I had to text her each morning to say how I was. She remained extremely worried throughout the pregnancy.

My childhood

The 70s and 80s

MUM was from a pig farm in County Wicklow, 25 miles from Glencullen, and had married my Dad, who was a sheep and cattle farmer. Farming was their life and they had their own special relationship: Mum was the boss in the house and Dad was the boss on the farm. They were married at an early age and, whatever chemistry their relationship exuded, it had kept them very much in love for what was going to be more than 50 years.

Mum was my world. She knew what was going on in the house and in her children's lives. Always remembering my friends' names and my relationships with them, was a testament of her love for me. She rarely judged people and wasn't into gossip. She was a good looking woman, and occasionally wore a little make-up which enhanced her features. Her gentle gestures, and her ability to put other people at ease in an empathetic way, were some of her charms.

However, we had one problem which incensed both her and me. Our fashion sense would sometimes differ and she found it difficult to accept that, from the age of three I knew what I wanted to wear. I put up great resistance when faced with some hideous pass-me-down dress or jumper, which she loved and I clearly didn't.

But our major falling out was always heightened when driving to Teresa's Hair Salon to get my hair cut. I wanted long hair but she didn't. She would blatantly tell Teresa to cut it short and I'd sit in the chair scowling.

Every so often I got my way, and when I was ten I somehow managed to keep my hair long. I remember saving up to buy cerise ribbons to wear in my pigtails and would steal hair-grips from my Granny's dressing table any time we were visiting.

'Mum will you put up my hair for school?' I'd say five mornings a week.

'Where's the brush? Have you the hair elastics?' she'd reply, starting to put the hairbrush through my tangled mass of thick hair.

I knew from her tone of voice and from her unimpressed face, she didn't like doing my hair which didn't help my cause one little bit. But I knew it suited me long.

When we were young she was strict yet approachable. If we were bold, she would shout and was a frightening woman to be around. One day when my sister, Carla, refused to eat her dinner, Mum lost all reason and poured the mince and carrots into the bin. She would warn us and warn us and then erupt like a sudden geyser breaking through ice. I used to remain mute in these situations and silently pleaded with my siblings to behave.

Consuming dinners could be fraught with anxiety for me too. I was a picky eater and was strongly encouraged to eat my food. Sometimes I sat alone trying to put morsels of egg into my mouth. The oily taste and texture, sliding down my throat wasn't pleasant, but after a while Mum would start to feel remorseful, give in and bargain with me. She was just too nice!

'If you eat three more forkfuls of omelette, you can have some custard.'

We always had a surplus amount of milk from our one milking-cow and Mum was an expert dessert maker. When I'd trudge in the door from school, I would go over to the Rayburn to see what milk-pudding was bubbling on the hot stove. Semolina, rice pudding, custard and corn-flour would all smell the same, so a quick investigation was necessary to ascertain the exact after-dinner treat.

Some days the smell of baking would engulf me before I even opened the door. There is nothing as nice as the smell of an apple-sponge cake, scones or buns which have been taken straight from the oven. Mum would generously spread the scones with butter and homemade raspberry jam and then lather on whipped cream. Delicious!

We all relied on her decisions but, when Mum and Dad were out farming Dad was the ultimate boss.

Born in 1933, he was a big, handsome man with a powerful voice and when he entered a room people felt his presence. He was a man of the earth and was reared with nature all around him. His innate knowledge of animals could be attributed to his parents who had a passion for the sheep, cattle, goats, dogs, cats and hens which roamed around the fields and the farmyard.

After the death of my grandfather, Dad inherited the family farm when he was 19-years-old. The house looked out over Dublin city – The Three Rock Mountain to the west, Howth to the north, and Killiney to the east. The farmyard was at the rear of the house and there were many disused dwellings where, in my grandfather's time, vagabond workers would have slept. The workers helped on the farm during busy times like hay-making or harvesting before they set off in search of more work.

There was a deep well and a little pond in the yard too. During the spring the pond was alive with frogspawn and we used to check to see if the spawn had turned into tadpoles.

I was making dams in the pond one day when I heard my father's voice.

'Climb up on the steps of the cow-house NOW!'

I scampered as fast as I could. This was serious. The Charolais bull, Tony (named after its previous owner), was let out for his daily exercise and drink from the pond. It was the most dangerous part of the farming day. The bull was cantankerous and unpredictable and would have had the ability to stamp you to death in a few seconds.

'Hurry up, you're so slow. Go!'

I slipped but didn't shout out when I felt the pain of a sharp-edged stone enter the flesh on my knee. I knew better. When Dad was shouting I morphed into the child I thought he wanted me to be. I pretended to be brave and tough. I was no longer girly or feminine. I did what I was told and I hid on the steps far away from the bull and his human alter-ego.

I was annoyed I had to help Dad that day. It was supposed to be Philip's turn but he was playing a rugby match in Rathmines and I was filling in for him.

I often vented my frustration at my younger brother, Philip. He had a special relationship with Mum and at times I envied their bond. He was a solid, hard-working boy and had an endearing, gentle manner. We all adored Philip, the baby, and it was the norm for him to have three sisters vying for his attention. I could find no fault in such a pacifist, so I would try to get a reaction from him by threatening to take money from his piggy-bank or steal some sweets from his Lenten box. But Philip rarely rose to my challenge, so I backed away and appreciated Philip for the self-contented brother he was.

I always preferred doing chores indoors rather than out on the farm. Newtown House, where Dad grew up, was a strong-farmer's house from Famine times. We too, were raised in this large house. It was typical of that era, a drawing-room on one side of the front door and an oversized dining-room on the other side. There was a small, cosy kitchen to the rear of the house.

The four bedrooms, of very disproportionate shape, were upstairs. My parents' room was hotel-sized, whilst my brother's room was just big enough for a single bed, a colossal black wardrobe and a Paddington Bear. My sisters and I also had our own bedrooms.

The eldest, Carla, was five years older than me, 5-feet-9 in height, slim, sallow-skinned and was often referred to as a 'stunner.' The most adventurous of my three siblings, she paved the way for us by testing boundaries with my parents. No matter what the rest of us did, it was never quite as bad as Carla's pursuit for independence.

Carla was only eight when one Monday morning, in an attempt to convince Mum she had a fever and couldn't go to school, she shattered a thermometer in a cup of hot chocolate, when she was supposedly taking her own temperature.

She was the first to accidently shatter the glass of my parents' bedroom window when she was hitting tennis balls with her much coveted John McEnroe racquet. It was she who crashed my parents' Fiat Ritmo by putting the car into reverse when parked against a wall. Carla was a beautiful, lovable rogue whose behaviour often frustrated my mother.

I looked up to my other sister, Ann, and wanted to be included in the fun she and her friends were having when they locked her bedroom door for 'serious chats'. She would shout at me to go away and found her younger sister annoying. I'd be the one who'd get her into trouble when she closed her bedroom door in my face.

In many ways Ann and I were physically similar. We were the same height, had thick, brown hair, our bone structure wasn't as defined as Carla's and following many years of orthodontic intervention, we too had straight teeth.

Our similarities stopped there. She was a natural sportswoman and was on the Irish-netball team in the mid-

80s. Although hockey, netball, gymnastics, athletics and cricket were compulsory sports in school, I was never a natural.

Ann adored farming and went to agricultural college after finishing school. I didn't. She loved messing around and horse-playing with our little brother: I was too pseudo-sophisticated to join in their 'immature' games.

More often than not we fought like only sisters can. She embarrassed me and I her. We were very different. I wore make-up on the farm and on snowy days, she would purposely arrive into school in her well-worn wellies, oblivious to the cow-dung on the sole of these boots. I'd be mortified and pretend I didn't know her.

But Ann was kind and thoughtful and she always looked out for me when we were in school. She cared for her family and epitimised the idiom that blood is thicker than water.

Friends and family visit us in Cyprus

2009

THE hot summer weather arrived, bringing my family, friends and Kieran's Mum to Cyprus for holidays. We weren't in a position to put them up in our house so we arranged that they would stay in holiday apartments close by. I needed my life to be as stress-free as possible and Kieran and I had to change from being very accommodating people to carefully accommodating people. It was probably our last chance at becoming parents and we found it difficult putting our needs before the needs of others, but for the sake of the ever growing baby, we'd little choice. He was our number one priority and I needed to be able to relax in my own home.

My two sisters visited for a week in May. I was excited in anticipation of their visit and my journey to the airport was a blur of exhilaration.

My hands trembled watching for them to exit the arrivals gate. It was wonderful seeing them as we hadn't seen one another for nine months. We were weepy and embraced for a long time.

'I can't believe my little sister's pregnant.' Ann said, studying my bump.

'We're all delighted for you and Kieran. I was so excited I just couldn't resist buying you this,' Carla said, handing me a bag with a wrapped present inside.

I opened the gift-bag and I saw little white babygros and tiny coloured socks.

Carla, forever generous.

'Wow! They're so cute!'

I became emotional and spluttered, 'The reality of having a baby is only just beginning to set in. We've been too afraid to buy anything for the baby and these first little items of clothing are beautiful. Thank you.'

'You're welcome. You and Kieran deserve this baby more than anyone.'

We were eager to show them our way of life in Cyprus so Kieran took some time off work and we toured different parts of the island.

'Let's go to the north today,' Kieran said, on an unusually overcast day.

Northern Cyprus was very different to the south. Turkish Cypriots controlled the north and there was a strong Muslim presence which could be witnessed from the pronouncement call-to-prayer five times a day from the minarets in the many mosques in the villages and towns.

We travelled across the border and went straight to Varosha (the ghost city). We got out of the car and walked onto a beach which stretched for miles in front of our eyes. Further along, we could see that the old city was barricaded off and a fence halted our beach-walk. Old wooden beach umbrellas stood forlornly on the other side of the barricade. How peculiar it was to see such a beautiful abandoned resort.

'Wow! What happened to the city?' Ann asked.

'Varosha used to be one of the most popular tourist areas in the world in the early 1970s. The rich and famous of the time like Liz Taylor and Brigitte Bardot holidayed here but it's been frozen in time.'

Derelict hotels from decades before were now standing eerily along the beach looking old and uncared for. Shabby curtains blew out of broken windows in the sea breeze.

Kieran continued, 'There were reports that inhabitants and hotel residents ran for their lives when the Turkish army invaded Cyprus thirty-five years ago.'

He was right. Everything was as it had been left. Time had stood still: it was still 1974.

Under the watchful eye of some Turkish military, Ann, Carla, Kieran and I remained transfixed on the unique sandy beach looking at the fenced off ghost city. We never took our cameras out of our handbags. There were signs saying 'No photography' and there's nothing as effective as men with rifles to make you obey the rules.

'This place gives me the shivers.'

Kieran was on a roll.

'Imagine looking out your window to see if it was safe to flee, before the Turkish military marched onto your streets and captured your city. Apparently dinners were left uneaten on tables, and windows left open as the people ran for their lives.'

There was so much ancient and modern history on the island. Our visitors were enthusiastic about what they saw and loved being shown around. When Kieran was working, Ann, Carla and I went for meals together and shared months of news.

A week later, I found it hard to say goodbye. The next time we would meet, I would be coming out of arrivals in Dublin with a little bundle of joy in my arms. It was exciting to think of the welcome-home party. Kieran and I had gone over as two and would be returning as three.

'Goodbye Ann and Carla. Thanks for coming over.'

'See you in five months,' Ann replied, with a warm grin which accentuated her cute dimples.

'Thanks for showing us around. You really have an amazing life here. I'm envious of the two of you,' Carla said, embracing me and following Ann into departures.

The golden sands of Nissi Beach in Ayia Napa had a certain appeal, and at weekends I often arranged to meet my friends, Sandra and Sinéad there. The due date of the birth of the baby was getting closer, and I rarely ventured far from the maternity hospital. Ayia Napa was the perfect distance from our house. From May to November the sun shone on the clear turquoise water of Nissi Beach and gave off a haze in sweltering heat. Sandra, Sinéad and I either huddled together under beach umbrellas or went to the beachfront tavern for ice-cream, disassociating ourselves from large groups of Irish and British teenagers who'd noisily arrive onto the beach in the late afternoon in poor condition, to sleep off the remnants of the night before.

Sandra was tall, dark haired and tanned. She was a member of An Garda and was based in Nicosia. I had been attracted to her warmth straight away – she drew me into her world of care, gossip and good-humour. It didn't take us long to become close friends. She was a kind and sympathetic person and was good fun to be around. She would often phone me during quiet times at work and we could chat for ages. Sometimes at the weekends when she wasn't working, she came to Pyla to escape the dead city-heat of the inland capital city and stayed with us in our house near the cooler sea-breeze. I always looked forward to her visits.

'I never want to go home to Ireland,' Sandra said one day when she, Sinéad and I were having our lunch under the shade of the awning of a beach tavern.

'Me neither. If only we could all stay another few months,' I replied, looking up at the two women.

'I'd have no problem staying another year,' Sinéad piped up. 'The new Irish group coming in August don't know how lucky they are.'

'Yeah, but would it become monotonous? Would we get lonely for our families?' I said, looking at them. 'Or maybe not.'

We eyed one another and smirked because we knew what each of us was thinking. There was great freedom being away from home – boredom and loneliness hadn't been an issue for any of us during the year.

But the end was approaching.

The birth of our child

COMING towards the end of each contingent's tour, a final farewell party was always held in the bar in the UNPA (United Nations Protected Area). There were many of these celebrations throughout the year which we had enthusiastically attended. The celebrations were called 'Mug-Outs.' Each police officer, whose contract was terminating, was presented with a silver-engraved mug as a keepsake of their UN mission in Cyprus. There were speeches and drinks, food and laughter.

Following the formalities, a PowerPoint presentation, made up of a collage of photos of the police men and women at work and of their social lives in Cyprus, were shown on a large screen in the bar.

Kieran was one of two Gardaí who took on the onerous task of compiling the Mug-Out PowerPoint presentation for the Irish Contingent and he spent time gathering photos from his colleagues who would be leaving in mid-August. The last weeks before I was due to give birth, he had devoted most evenings sourcing backing music which would complement the photo montage he had selected. *Coldplay, Snow Patrol* and *Stereophonics* were just some of the artists he chose.

'What do you think of this music?' Kieran, ever the perfectionist, asked me again.

He was putting a lot of work into the presentation. An Garda Síochána was an important institution in Kieran's eyes – he was proud to be a member of the Force and was forever loyal to the organisation.

'It's great but would these photos be better here?' I replied.

We bandied about whether a picture should be added or omitted and, as we discussed the quality, meaning and validity of each individual photo, the selected music was playing in the background. *The Farm* very appropriately opened the PowerPoint.

'*Altogether now*

Altogether now

Altogether now in no man's land...'

He replayed the songs continuously for weeks, and I'm sure our little baby was sick to death hearing the same repetitive music.

I wasn't. I loved every beat, rhythm, lyric, and each song held a special place in my heart. The music was always going to be a reminder of the fun times and friendships we had in Cyprus. It was nostalgia at its best and was going to bring tears to my eyes for many years to come, when the great happy memories would be drowned by immense sadness.

But for now the music represented the end of Kieran's tour of work in Cyprus and the approaching birth of our baby.

Dr Kassinis planned to carry out a Caesarean section under general anaesthetic on Friday July 24. Like most expectant mothers, I'd had ideals throughout the pregnancy and had wanted a natural birth. But at the end of the day a live birth was what it boiled down to. However that happened.

Friday morning arrived and there was calm in our house. I was organised and had everything ready from the weeks before; one baby bag, one Mummy bag and one Daddy overnight bag. Numerous items had been crossed off my list every time I'd packed, unpacked and repacked. The bag now contained three new nighties, a dressing gown and some matching nursing-bras, all white in colour and with bands of baby-blues and pinks around the edges. There were new batteries in the camera, I was waxed to an inch of my life, my toe nails were painted red and my hair was immaculately straight. I wasn't going to look haggard in those first post-baby photos. The Moses basket, pram and car-seat had been proudly taken out of their boxes, instructions read and were set up ready for the baby's home-coming.

'Are you ready Kim?'

'I'm just taking one last look at the house.'

'Let's go. Come on, it's nearly seven. Into the car.'

The car's air conditioning was up high on an already hot summer's morning. As we were speeding down the road towards Larnaca, my heart was pounding.

I'm going to be a mother. At last!

All of a sudden we arrived at the hospital. I was deep in thought and I got out of the car slowly.

'Are you OK?' Kieran asked.

'I think so. The whole thing is just mind-blowing.'

He came over to me and we hugged each other tightly.

73

'It will all go fine. You and the baby will be fine.'

We went up to the first floor and I approached the Nurses' Station.

'Kalimera, I'm booked in with Dr Kassinis.'

'Follow me please.'

The same room I had been in some months before in this hospital no longer seemed as threatening as it had been when I'd thought I was going to miscarry. I was now so close to giving birth and my excitement was starting to out-weigh my anxiety.

'Will you put on this gown and we'll come and get you in twenty minutes?' the nurse asked, before closing the door behind her.

The blue disposable-gown discretely covered the front of my body, but that was about it. Visions of Jack Nicholson in his hospital gown, trundling down a corridor in *Something's Got to Give* came to mind, and as I was carrying an extra two and a half stone in weight, the resemblance was sure to be uncanny.

Luckily (unlike Nicholson) I didn't have to walk. I was brought up to theatre on a trolley.

Saying goodbye was in the eye-contact Kieran and I tenderly shared with one other. We were both going to be on our own for the next little while and it felt daunting.

I let go Kieran's hand and watched him walk back down the corridor.

This is it. I'm alone. It's not right. Kieran should be with me. What if something goes wrong? Come back, this baby is for the two of us.

The theatre was a cold sterile room with stainless steel equipment everywhere I looked. There seemed to be nurses and doctors all around me. They were dressed in blue gowns tied over green scrubs and were chatting to one another through white surgical masks and ignoring me, the patient, lying on the operating table.

About an hour later, I could vaguely hear a nurse's voice.

'It's all over now, wake up. Kim, wake up.'

I heard the same badgering from Kieran.

'Wake up Kim, you've been great, you've had the baby.'

I tried to open one eye and I could see the new proud Daddy cradling our baby.

'Is it a boy, Kieran?'

'Yes we have a beautiful little boy.'

I looked at my baby for the first time. He was tiny, he was perfect and he was ours. His blond hair was as golden as Kieran's, and his contrasting sallow skin made him look truly adorable. Kieran laid him on my chest. He positioned him close to my breast to suckle, but the baby just rubbed his gorgeous little nose on me. I wasn't concerned, not all babies are hungry when they are born.

A month prior, we had attended an antenatal course in Dhekelia (a UK sovereign base in Cyprus) with some spouses of the men in the British Forces. The midwives had shown me the technique of breast feeding – a practice which had been vehemently supported by them.

Later, when our baby was sleeping in my arms, Kieran turned on the flat-screen TV in the room. He flicked through the channels and stopped.

'Oh my God, look at this!'

One of the channels showed babies in the nursery just three rooms down the corridor from mine. There were four dark-haired Cypriot babies in little cots. We could see a paediatric nurse change the babies' nappies and feed bottles to them.

'Why aren't the mothers doing that? Are they not breast feeding?' I asked. 'How come the babies aren't in the room with them?'

I was perplexed by what I saw and I became even more protective of our little one. I was coping well on my own and couldn't take my eyes off my baby. Why would the women deprive themselves of this privilege?

It was 37°C outside, when we proudly brought Dylan, our baby, into our house for the very first time. Kieran placed him gently in the new Moses basket in the sitting room. I looked at Dylan in awe: I knew our lives couldn't get any better than this. We were a family at last. We had the little baby we had always wanted and it was a very special time.

The whole experience of being a new mother was incredibly overwhelming. My life had changed in such a positive way. I craved Dylan's company and loved the quiet times alone with my baby. He'd lie on my chest or on the bed and I was mesmerised by both him and by nature. It was a time for us to be together – time of bonding.

Dylan woke and I lifted him to my breast to feed. The defunct steriliser which was sitting forlornly in its box caught my eye.

You can stay in that box for a while yet. I've this under control. I'm not bottle-feeding my baby.

The following three days were magical. We lived as a family in our home and during the day Kieran and I slept in single beds and Dylan slept in the Moses basket between us. The windows were open and I can distinctly remember a sea breeze infiltrating the bedroom. They were exceptional days. Our house was full of love.

On Friday, a week after Dylan's birth, one of the midwives from the British Forces came to visit us at home. We weren't part of the Forces but nevertheless she had kindly taken time off work to offer me post-natal support.

'It's beautiful here,' she said, sitting in the shade near the pool eating Carina's homemade scones and drinking tea. 'We aren't used to this type of living. Many army houses resemble each other and the compounds are more or less the same. It's lovely to pay a visit to someone in a house outside of the Army Base.'

'Yes we are lucky to be in Cyprus. We've loved every minute of it,' I said.

'When are you going back to Ireland?'

'We haven't booked our flights yet. The rest of the Irish Contingent will be gone by the end of August, but we're definitely going to holiday on the island for a few weeks. We're heading to Pissouri next week with our baby. Mum's coming over then, to see Dylan and then we'll book flights to go home maybe six weeks' later.'

'You'll probably be met by a fanfare of family who'll be dying to see Dylan.'

'I think that's what they're planning, alright.'

I was excited by thoughts of our return and the homecoming which would ensue.

That evening we went for dinner on the seafront in Larnaca and instead of our usual 'people watching,' we spoke non-stop about our son. Other people's appearance, demeanour and sense of dress went over our heads. We were too consumed with our bundle of joy.

It was exciting to show off our baby in public and to push the new pram. I could dress Dylan up, play with him and would be walking around Larnaca and Pyla with my baby, and when I'd return home to Ballina - Killaloe I'd do the very same.

We ordered large ice-creams and walked hand in hand along the promenade. We no longer looked like novices. An aura of confidence and experience was starting to ooze from us.

'I'm stuffed. I think it's time to go,' I said, wiping chocolate off my lips. 'I can't believe Dylan's not hungry again, he didn't take much at his last feed.'

'Speak of the devil.'

I looked into the pram and watched Dylan stretch his arms to the sides. His face started to contort and I knew he needed to be fed.

'We'll keep going and I'll feed him when we get back.'

The house was very warm when we got home and Kieran opened the upstairs windows. I got undressed, clambered into bed and set my pillows straight. I reached out for Kieran to hand me Dylan.

'I'm not quite as sore as I was during the week,' I commented to Kieran when Dylan had latched on. 'Or maybe it's taken the week to get used to it.'

'I'll take Dylan tonight and you have a good night's sleep.'

When the feed was over I yawned, 'I'm wrecked. I'm going to go asleep. I left a bottle of expressed milk in the fridge for his feed later.'

'Goodnight my two precious family members,' Kieran said, kissing us both on the lips.

'Goodnight Daddy. We love you.'

Within two hours my life was going to change forever.

Part
Two

I can't see you — who is it?

I COULD hear voices at different times. Kieran was whispering and was telling me how much he loved me. It felt comforting hearing such sentiments and I loved him even more. He told me about Dylan, our son, what he was doing, and what a fantastic mother I was. As time went by and some hours had passed, I grew curious. We'd been together seventeen years and were still very much in love, however, even I who thrives on expressions like 'I love you' was wondering why he was repeatedly using such beautiful words.

'I'll be back soon, Assumpta,' I heard Kieran say.

Assumpta? That's my Mum!

Sleep.

Sometime later I sensed my mother close-by and asked her where I was. My voice was very soft and I had to repeat the question, 'Where am I?'

'Shush, just sleep pet.'

'Mum, where am I?'

'You're in ICU, in Nicosia General Hospital, love.'

'Why are you in Cyprus?'

'You're a little sick and I had to be with you. Ann is also here. Good girl, you need to sleep.'

She tried to sound casual and I accepted her reply. The thought of my sister and mother being in Cyprus with me didn't register as unusual. I was so excited about them seeing my new baby that everything else faded into oblivion.

'Did you see him? Isn't he beautiful?' I asked.

'Shush now.'

'Did you see him?'

'Kim, he's just fantastic! How are you feeling?'

'Fine,' I replied dismissively. I only wanted to talk about her newest grandson and I'd no interest in talking about myself. 'He's blond like Kieran.'

I'm not sure if other women do this when they are expecting, but secretly I had a list of features I hoped my child would inherit – his father's hair colour had been top of that list.

I started to sob.

Where was my baby? Why were we separated?

I slept.

I could hear my sister, Ann, talking to me as I started to wake but I couldn't see her.

'How are you Kimmy? I'm also here to be with you.'

My head is sore, I can't open my eyes. I can't see anyone.

Sleep.

After some time I heard my Dad's voice.

'How's my lady?' He was squeezing my index finger with his large coarse hand. I knew he was upset so I tried to comfort him by holding onto his finger. I never wanted to let go. He was my Dad – he'd fix whatever was wrong. I trusted him to. He always had before.

My God, what's going on?

Sleep.

My other sister, Carla, came in a while later or was it a day or a week after? Time was indiscernible.

'Who's there?'

'It's me Kim. It's Carla.'

'Did you see Dylan?'

'Hush now. Don't talk.'

'Did you see Dylan?'

'Sorry Kim, I can't hear you.'

I tried one more time.

'Dylan, did you see him?'

'Yes I did. He's gorgeous, just like his Mum.'

She squeezed my hand and I knew she cared.

'Will you be his godmother?'

'Can you say that again, I can't hear?'

She leant closer to me and I repeated my question.

'I'd love to be. I'd be honoured.'

I think she may have cried and I knew she was touched by my request.

I felt bad I hadn't asked Ann to be Dylan's godmother, so later when next I heard her voice I felt I'd to break the news to her, and reason that on a numerical basis she had more godchildren than Carla, and as a cost-saving measure she should be relieved not to have been asked.

I was afraid of her reaction in case she was hurt. I need not have been. She told me not to worry and that she really loved me. Those words of love were frightening. Whilst we are a demonstrative family, we don't express love for each other so vehemently.

Kieran's brother and sister (Fergal and Laura) came into my room to visit too, two minutes, two hours or two days later.

I didn't think their presence odd either. When I heard Kieran's older sister speaking beside my bed I felt touched she had travelled to be with Kieran and me. She has three adorable children and I was pleased my little boy carried a slight resemblance to her boys.

'He's so gorgeous and really good. You're amazing to have given birth to such a beautiful boy,' she said.

I was chuffed.

'Does he look like your kids?'

It was a rhetorical question.

I could feel Laura hesitate, flustered – trying to work what to say.

I needed to help her so I said, 'I think he does. He's just so cute like your boys.'

I was coaxing an affirmative answer from her.

'Yes he looks very like them when they were born.'

Phew! That awkward conversation is over.

Fergal started to speak in a soft voice. His kind words of reassurance flitted in and out of my head for days to come. I wondered why my younger brother-in-law sounded so concerned about my well-being and why he was trying to comfort me.

I drifted into sleep.

'I'm hungry,' I tried to say when I woke sometime later.

Mum and Kieran were by my bedside and they jumped up in alarm.

'What did you say, love?'

'Mum, where am I?'

'What, Kim?'

'I'm hungry.'

I could hear the slurring in my voice but was determined to get some food, so I persisted, 'I'm hungry.'

'I think she's hungry,' Mum said to Kieran.

'What would you like to eat?'

'Where am I?'

'You're in the hospital opposite The Mall of Cyprus where you and the girls used to go shopping.'

'IKEA?'

'Yes, opposite IKEA.' Kieran laughed. 'You'll always remember where the shops are!'

'Get me a chocolate fondant,' I murmured.

'What? I can't hear you.'

I repeated, 'A chocolate fondant. Chocolate cake.'

'You want a chocolate fondant? But I don't know where to get one.'

'IKEA.'

'They sell furniture in IKEA,' he said softly. 'Will I go to Costa Coffee?'

'IKEA,'

Are they stupid? We'd eaten in IKEA during the year and the fondants there were gorgeous.

'IKEA!' I repeated louder.

'Oh, in the restaurant?'

'Uh hum.'

'I'll ask the doctor if you're allowed to eat.'

I waited and then smelled some food approach my bed. My head hurt and I'd to keep my eyes shut.

'The doctor said you can eat a little of this. Open your mouth and I'll feed you.'

'What is it?'

'Some grilled chicken and white rice,' he said, putting a little in my mouth.

But he was too slow and I had to take over.

'I'll do it. No, I don't want a fork.'

Fistfuls of boiled rice and morsels of chicken were not enough to satisfy my hunger.

'Slow down, Kim, you'll make yourself sick. You haven't eaten in days and your stomach mightn't be up to it,' Kieran explained.

I hadn't time to listen. I was ravenous. My hand was searching for the plate and each time I felt the heat of the food, I stuffed more food into my mouth.

'That's probably enough now,' a woman, presumably a nurse, said.

I felt she was trying to withdraw the tray. I held onto the precious food which was safe in my grasp, shoved it into my mouth and reached out for more. I failed. I didn't know where the plate was.

'Where's the cake?'

'You can have some tomorrow.'

'I want it now.'

'You can't Kimmy,' Mum explained.

'What happened to me?'

'Sorry Kim, I don't know what you're saying.'

'What happened?'

'You'd a little bleed in your brain.'

'I don't understand.'

'You'd a bleed, but you're getting better now. You're doing great.'

'Why can't I feel my arm?'

'It's not working.'

I paused.

I hadn't the wherewithal to digest this information so I ignored the enormity of what she said and continued, 'I can't move my leg.'

'I know. Your left side is paralysed at the moment but the doctors say you'll get better.'

I slept.

For how long, I didn't know.

I'm so confused

THERE were bars around me, jailing me. I attempted to rock back and forth but I only managed a little movement on one side of my body. I opened my eyes and saw the blurred green light of an exit sign over a door. I thought I was in a hospital. Partially delirious, but partially awake, I kept mumbling, 'Take the bars away. I want to get out of this bed. Let me out!'

No one was awake to hear my pleas so I lay still trying to get some sleep. But sleep evaded me.

I was waiting for something to happen and the confusion was awakening within me again. Was it day or night? I thought it was bright outside but in the month of August in Cyprus the sun rises at 4 a.m. The cloudless-blue sky on the other side of the window was telling me nothing. My mind started to drift again. All of this thinking was taking too much from me and I shut my eyes and slept.

When I woke, vague memories of hearing my family came rolling in.

Yes, I'm right. I'm in hospital. I think my family are somewhere close by or am I dreaming?

I looked around. I could see there were four beds in the ward. Two women were getting themselves into a sitting position. They smiled at me and I closed my eyes pretending I didn't see them.

As I was battling with my thoughts, I noticed breakfast had been served. The smell of coffee was arousing me from drowsiness. I wasn't sure how or when it arrived but I observed the other patients buttering bread. I was hungry and wanted to taste the delights the morning had brought. I turned my head slightly and I noticed a tray sitting on the windowsill to the left of me.

Ouch, my head.

The sun was blazing through the closed windows. It was probably going to be 36°C by lunchtime. I stretched my hand to reach my breakfast but my arm refused to move. Instead I sat back and over a period of time I watched the corners of the forbidden bread curl up to reach the sun.

Why was no one handing the tray to me? Where's Dylan?

I gave up trying to get the tray and my mind started to drift and I hoped someone I knew would visit and explain why I was in a hospital. I was too ill to understand what was going on.

The sound of some female voices came closer and I looked up to see two young nurses approach my bed.

'Good morning Kim, how are you?' one of them asked standing to the left of me.

It hurt my head to turn and I glanced at her wondering how she knew my name.

'I tried to get out of bed, but I can't. Is it still night time? I couldn't sleep, the night was so long.' I said to her colleague who was to the right of me.

'It's 7.30 a.m.'

Oh thank God. But where is my baby? He must be nearby somewhere.

These morning angels reassured me that the dreadful night was over. The beautiful nurses chatted and told me their names were Stella and Katharyn, and that they were both 20-year-old nursing students. They showed enthusiasm and compassion in their zest for learning their trade. Dark silky hair co-ordinated with their unblemished sallow-skin and the hue of blue uniforms complimented the white teeth of their smiles. I couldn't tell them apart. It didn't matter. They came as a pair and I liked them as a couple. They were in good form and tried to practise their English on me.

'How old is you?'

'Thirty-nine,' I muttered.

I watched them eye-ball each other in surprise and I was mistakenly complimented by their semblance of surprise.

They think I look young for my age. A year lying under the sun's rays mustn't have caused too much skin damage. Where's Dylan, I can't see him?

But in truth they were shocked that someone my age was battling for their life.

'I've a clean nightdress for you, but first I cleaning you with sponge. Have you soap?'

'I don't know.'

'I find some.'

The moisture of the sponge on my body felt good and I lay flat on the bed in a child-like way, allowing my carers to

91

nurture me. They dressed me in a black, cotton nightie, one I'd never seen before and I wondered where my new pretty maternity night-clothes were.

They rolled me on my side and deftly removed the bottom sheet from under me. Their innocuous banter and giggles were refreshing and helped me forget about the pain I was in. I wanted them to stay with me forever.

Following their departure, I watched some of the goings-on around me as some middle-aged women went in and out of the bathroom with their towels and wash-bags to prepare for the day ahead. Lying there watching them, I wondered why I wasn't doing the same? They were chatting and seemed to be in a routine and I felt excluded. I wanted to go towards the bathroom and chit-chat with them but I found it hard to move.

'Hi Kim,' a girl to the right of me said.

The voice was that of a young woman, maybe in her late teens who was visiting the patient lying in the bed next to mine. I hadn't noticed her before.

'Hi.'

The young woman leaned towards me.

'My sister has broken her back. She fell down stairs and her three-year-old phoned an ambulance. She's to lie here for eight weeks without moving.'

'Your poor sister! That's a terrible thing to happen.'

Imagine breaking your back! At least nothing that bad happened to me. I'll be better tomorrow and when I find Dylan, things will go back to normal.

I was drifting in and out of a restless sleep, trying to ignore the pounding in my head when I heard Kieran arrive into the ward.

'That girl,' I whispered, pointing to my right, 'has broken her back.'

'I know. I've spoken to her sister and mother a few times.'

'But it's awful for her. She has a child.'

'Yes it is. How are you?'

'My head's hurting so much that I can't sleep. Where's Dylan?'

'I can't hear you, say it again.'

'Who has Dylan? My head's sore.'

'I'll get something for it.'

When the paracetemol tablets arrived I refused to take them, remembering that women who breast-feed shouldn't take medication as it contaminates their milk supply. I had to keep my body free of all toxins because I was nursing my little boy.

Instead, I lifted my right hand to the source of the pain in my head. All I could feel was stubble where my long brown hair used to be. Little fragments of dry, clotted blood were crumbling from my scalp into my fingers. Nothing was making any sense.

Where's my hair gone? Why's my head sore?

I looked at Kieran.

'Do you love him?' I asked.

'Who?

'Dylan.'

'Yes, I love Dylan very much.'

93

'But do you really love him?' I laboured the question.

It was so important to me Kieran loved our son for the two of us. I hadn't seen my baby for so long and my heart was breaking. I was unable to stroke and hold Dylan and tell him he was the most important person in my live. I needed Kieran to tell my son that his Mummy would be home soon, but for the moment Kieran needed to doubly love Dylan for us both.

'Tell him I love him so much. I really want to see him. Bring him in,' I sobbed hysterically.

'Of course I will Kim, now get some sleep before the nurse brings you downstairs for an x-ray. Carla will be coming in soon and I'll see you this afternoon. I need to go back to bed as I was up most of the night feeding Dylan and trying to get him back asleep. He's been crying a lot because I think he might be constipated.'

Maybe he's missing his Mummy.

He said his goodbyes and I was alone again. My head was spinning and I dozed until a vibration under my body alerted me something different was happening.

A trolley! I'm on a trolley. Kieran had mentioned something about a nurse and going downstairs. Why am I leaving the ward? Oh God, I'm going for an x-ray.

I started shaking anxiously and tried hard to catch someone's attention. My attempts were in vain. My voice was too weak, I was shouting soundlessly, 'Please stop! I'm wearing an underwired bra. The metal is going to burn through my skin during the x-ray.'

It was like something from a horror movie. No-one could hear me shout, as in truth I could not be heard. I tried to use my eyes to catch someone's attention but I couldn't really open them. It hurt too much.

I tried grunting. Eventually I caught the attention of a nurse. She leant over me breathing garlic in my face and tried to hear what I was saying. She couldn't understand me so instead she dismissively endeavoured to reassure me I was fine.

Listen to me. No, don't walk away. Come back!

All of a sudden there was a bright light. The trolley was moving again and I could see the doors of the x-ray room were now open. I became more and more distressed.

They don't care if I burn to death.

Carla appeared from somewhere, held my hand and took time to work out what was causing her little sister to be so upset.

'Your bra has been removed,' she said, putting my mind to rest. 'It was taken off a few days ago.'

Thank God. They've no idea how scared I am.

When I woke sometime later, I was back in my bed. It was dark and I looked around for Carla but she was gone. The silence in the ward gave me time to think.

Under my hospital-gown my breasts were aching and my natural urge was to allow my baby to feed on the milk that was causing the pain. My head was throbbing and I tried to deliberate what was happening but I was battling with confusion. I needed clarity.

95

What have you done with my baby?

THE moring angels arrived to my bedside.

'Are you late today?' I asked the two young nurses.

'We are ten minutes late, that's all Kim,' said Stella, or was it Katharyn?

'The night is so long and I need to see your faces to know it's the morning, I get frightened.'

'OK Kim, tomorrow we will try come early at 7.15 a.m.'

'Thanks Stella.'

'No, I'm Katharyn not Stella. Remember I have much fat.'

They smirked at each other.

'I don't think you're fat.'

'Thank you. Can you lift your right arm so I will takes off your nightdress?'

When Katharyn removed my nightie I noticed bandaging around my breasts. White-coloured bandages were stretched tightly around my back flattening my newly-acquired-voluptuous boobs.

'Why is there bandaging?'

They looked at each other and I could tell they were unsure how much they were allowed to disclose to me. I asked them again and their innocent defences started to crumble. (Informing patients of their condition and prognosis had obviously not yet been covered as part of their nursing degree). They started to divulge.

'You were screaming in Intensive Care,' Stella said. 'The doctor get pump and taked the milk out.'

Katharyn's English was not quite as fluent as Stella's, but she was on a roll so she continued, 'The bandage make sure you no milk.'

I listened in horror. This barbaric procedure was invasive and uncalled for. Reality began to hit me.

My breasts are now empty because of an uncalled-for savage intervention. Because the Cypriots aren't into the whole breast-feeding thing, I'm being punished for my involvement. How am I going to be able to feed my baby and give him the 'best of breast'?

I want to feed him for six months. My baby has only received seven days of my milk. I've failed my new son and mother-kind all around the world. My baby is being fed formula – my plans had been so different. Why aren't I there looking after him?

I looked away to hide my tears and waited for the whistle-blowers to leave.

'How are you doing? It's nice to see you,' Kieran said, stepping aside allowing Stella and Katharyn exit the ward.

I started to quiz him to see if the two girls were right in what they had disclosed. He'd barely time to reply to my questioning when I blurted, 'I can express. It will start the milk flowing again. I can reverse formula-feeding back to breast-feeding. It will work.'

I didn't hear his explanation because sleep engulfed me yet again.

We had the same conversation about an hour later when I woke.

He tried to look excited.

'That's a good idea.'

'But I can, really I can.' I persisted, sensing his lack of enthusiasm.

He smiled sweetly.

'We'll see, maybe you can resume feeding Dylan in a few days' time when the medication is stopped.'

I had no idea why there were drugs in my body, all I knew was that I had given birth to a baby boy and he was not with me.

Sleep.

'Where's Dylan?' I asked, opening my weary eyes and noticing Kieran's empty arms.

'Laura and Fergal are minding him.'

'Why? What are your brother and sister doing here?' I said, forgetting I'd heard their voices a few days before.

Kieran was serious and said something about a brain surgery. It was a conversation I didn't want to hear or be part of, so I slept once again.

When I woke I peeked out from the side of my eye and watched as Kieran produced a diary from his pocket. He wanted to go through various dates with me, to see how disorientated I was (or wasn't). There were dates written in an old copybook and pointing to the first page, he asked me what happened on that particular Friday. I looked at him in horror! I will always remember what happened on Friday, July 24. It was the most amazing day of my life.

'Kim, tell me what happened.' His voice sounded urgent.

'Dylan was born on that day.'

Next he pointed to another date where he'd written something else.

'On Wednesday the three of us went out for lunch.'

All I could see were blurred words highlighted with fluorescent yellow and pink markers. My head spun. This exercise was really frustrating,

'Stop! I can't do this anymore.'

'Of course. We can do it another day, but I need to talk to you about something else. You're Dylan's Mummy so the decision is totally yours. We think Dylan's formula needs to change because he's getting constipated.'

We think? Who thinks?

'OK, you know best,' I said, knowing that Kieran was on top of things, but feeling hurt that this parenting issue was being discussed by others.

'Also, we feel he needs a soother to help him sleep. It can take a while for us to settle him and maybe a soother could help.'

That 'we' word again.

'Why does he need a soother?'

I had planned not to use soothers if at all possible.

'It's your decision.'

I knew that absolutely everyone was doing their best for Dylan and I was grateful they were doing feeds, changing nappies, bathing him and cuddling him. Kieran couldn't have done without their help. Their help allowed him spend time with his wife and with his baby – albeit in different cities.

'I don't really want him to have a soother. What do you think?'

'He's upset after each feed and not settling at all, but it's up to you.'

I believed him when he said "it's up to you" and I knew if I said no, he'd respect my wishes. However, deep down I knew I'd no choice. I wasn't in a position to comfort my baby who was in pain, so I'd to accept the collective advice I was being given. But I couldn't help feeling my plans were being sabotaged.

How did young unmarried girls feel in times past when nuns took their new-borns from them? How utterly inadequate did these girls feel when they weren't seen fit to care for their off-spring?

Because I wasn't well, I was being somewhat ostracised from the rearing of my own child. This was the start of two years of people (with the best will in the world) taking Dylan from me.

'OK, that's fine. I probably would have given him one at some stage anyway. Where is he?'

'Your Mum has him. She's in the house helping with the packing.'

'What packing?'

'They're flying home tomorrow.'

'Who?'

'Your Dad, Ann, Carla, my brother and sister.

'But I'm not better yet. Tell them to stay.'

'I'm sorry Kim I can't. They need to get back to work. I'll be here beside you until you're better. I'll not leave you alone. Neither your Mum nor I will leave.'

Very soon, too soon, the others were saying goodbye. I was still drifting in and out of heavy sleep and it was beginning to dawn on me that I was very ill.

How can you all abandon me in my hour of need? I'm not better yet and I need you to stay until I am. I want to be up and about before anyone goes home.

I felt a similarity between Jesus and me, as his apostles slept and abandoned him in the Garden of Gethsemane 2,000 years before.

Why have you forsaken me?

The words of a hymn we used to sing during Easter week in school replayed over in my head.

My soul is sad,

My heart is breaking tonight.

Could you not stay and comfort me until night?

...Could you not stay one hour with me?

I was alone and the pain of their departure stayed with me for a long time. Kieran was reassuring me that he and Mum were staying, but I didn't know if I could trust him. My rational thinking was gone. Too pre-occupied with myself, I couldn't understand what was going on. These five people had generously put their own lives on hold for nearly a week. Of course they needed to go home.

Whilst we will be forever grateful to them and to so many others for their selflessness, at that time I felt I'd been deserted.

Terror in hospital

'WHAT do you want now?' A male nurse demanded, approaching my bed.

'I don't know,' I whispered.

'You've pressed the bell two times already tonight. You have to stop.'

I put my hand to my head.

'I'm so confused. I don't know what's happening.'

He looked at me in disgust and annoyance, as though I was suffering from some kind of psychiatric illness which warranted disregard.

'Stop ringing the bell! I'm busy with other patients.'

He left and I was cross with myself for upsetting this nurse, who in all probability had chosen the wrong career. But I was lonely. I was afraid. I needed someone kind to mind me.

I pressed the bell.

No one came.

I pressed the bell again.

They're all refusing to come. I want to go home to Dylan. I'm supposed to be there with him.

'Kim, what's wrong?'

At last. It was Anna. I liked her.

'I don't know what's happening to me, Anna.'

'You're sick, but you will get better. It's 3 a.m. and you need to sleep. Is your head sore?'

'Yes,' I pretended.

Paracetamol was my new friend and helped me to go into a slumber. I was no longer keeping my body free of toxins, so when no one was looking, I had taken three tablets earlier with my supper. In the morning I would start to save the day's supply and take them just before I was to go to sleep that night. Washing the tablets down my throat with some water, I began to relax. I was happy Anna had come to my bedside to offer me some compassion. I was a vulnerable child who needed minding.

The drugs worked and I slept until Kieran arrived.

'How did you sleep?' he asked concerned, when he saw my eyes welling up.

'Please stay with me tonight. I'm so scared.'

I knew I was asking a lot of a father of a new-born baby but the nights were terrifying me. Kieran had never been one to survive well without sleep, and now I was knowingly killing him, but I'd never been so scared in all my life. I needed him.

'Of course I will.'

'I'm so sorry, I know you've Dylan to feed but I'm petrified. When I can sleep my dreams are of dragons and snakes, and then I wake and think I'm losing my mind. That awful male nurse certainly thinks so anyway.'

'We're in this together. The three of us are in it together.'

I looked at the bags under Kieran's eyes and I could smell his body odour, presumably from rushing around in the heat and driving at speed to get to me early. I knew he was under severe pressure. My heart heaved and I felt remorse.

'I'm sorry Kieran for asking you.'

'Don't be so ridiculous, Kim, it's not your fault. I love you for giving us Dylan, for taking such precious care of him for nine months. You're an amazing person. Dylan and I love you so much.'

He was compassionate in all he said.

'Can you remember the first time you felt Dylan kick?'

The first flutters in my stomach had happened very early one morning and because I wasn't sure what exactly it was, I had gone back to sleep. The same fluttering woke me an hour later and I had put Kieran's hand on my tummy so he too could experience the phenomenal work of nature.

'Wasn't it magical?' I replied.

I had never thought I'd be in a privileged position to experience such a sensation of a baby moving in my womb, and it had been wonderful.

A misty film of moisture started again in my eyes as I lay thinking of that special time. Our conversation was interrupted.

'Hello Kim.'

Kieran and I looked towards the end of my bed at an entourage of doctors and nurses who had come into the ward unnoticed by us.

'Oh, hello! These are the neurosurgeons who saved your life,' Kieran explained to me.

My eyesight had fully returned and I could see their silhouettes, which were temporarily blocking the sun. One of the doctors drew the curtains around us, and the area darkened slightly, making it easier for me to see the group. Three consultants wearing green scrubs, two student doctors in white coats, and a nurse, had all huddled into the tiny space by my bed. Kieran and I were outnumbered by medical professionals, who by their sheer volume in number were instilling confidence in me.

Surely one of you has a cure.

'How are you?' the most important-looking surgeon asked me.

He was closest to me and the rest of the team were listening attentively to him.

'This is Dr. Buros,' Kieran explained. 'He and these two other neurosurgeons operated on your brain.'

Dr Buros' small stature didn't take from the air of authority he was giving off. A bare scalp shone through balding hair and the thick dark stubble on his face made me think he'd been working through the night. He was looking at me and I had no idea what he was going to say.

'You're a lucky woman. We didn't know if you would live. It was touch and go for you but the surgery went very well and we are pleased.'

He looked over and smiled in a congratulatory way at the other two surgeons whose body language changed, backs arched, displaying pride in a job well done.

He took a pen out of his breast pocket and he started to poke various parts of the left side of my body with the tip of the lid.

'Can you feel the pen scraping along your foot?'

'No.'

'Can you feel me tapping your arm?'

'No.'

Again he looked at the other medics who were watching me closely. They conversed in Greek, glanced at me periodically and then at each other. My mind went to another place, a place I was getting accustomed to visiting – an ordinary place with ordinary people getting on with their ordinary lives, far away from the extraordinary goings on by my hospital bed.

'Can you move your foot?'

I willed my foot to move but it disobeyed.

'Can you move your arm?'

'Can you lift your leg?'

'Can you wriggle your toes?'

My body was in lock-down, defying me.

'No.'

More discussion.

'Don't worry, you will be walking in eight weeks.' Dr Buros said.

Eight weeks? That's forever.

I nodded.

'Have you any pain?'

'Yes, I can't sit up or move because the pain in the muscles in my bottom is shooting up and down my leg. Also, I'm sore here,' I said, pointing to my lower abdomen.

'Here?' he asked, lifting my nightie and examining my C-section scar.

'I don't think so,' I said. 'I'm not really sure where the pain's coming from.'

'The scar is healing well but we'll get a gynaecologist to see you. Maybe you've an infection from the birth.'

(E-coli in my bladder, due to the insertion and use of a catheter was going to go undiagnosed for a month and it would take four courses of antibiotics to clear it up.)

A nurse was awkwardly balancing paper on a clip-board, frantically writing something and looking intently from her notes to the doctor.

'What pain relief is she on?' I guessed the neurosurgeon said to her in Greek.

He may have told her to increase the dose because she nodded at him and returned to note-taking.

'I hear you haven't had a bowel-movement yet.'

'No, not in over two weeks,' the nurse replied for me.

'OK, let's go,' Dr Buros said to his colleagues.

Their rounds to my bedside were daily but unfortunately neither feeling nor movement returned to the left side of my body.

Carina, don't go !

'HI Kim.'

I looked up and saw my friend Carina who was a little flustered as she side-stepped one of the doctors. Her healthy looking glow lit up my bedside, and following the exit of the dour faces of the medics, her presence was a very welcome distraction.

'I'm going to go over to the shopping centre for a coffee. Will you stay here for a while until I come back?' Kieran asked Carina and he stood up to go.

'Yes, I'll be here,' she replied, watching Kieran go out the door.

When we were on our own she whispered, 'Was that one of your doctors I bumped into on my way in?'

'He's very handsome. I didn't know where to look when he was feeling my paralysed limbs and nodding to himself.'

'Yeah, and he's a bit too old for you!' She replied giving me one of her warm smiles.

She pulled out a chair to the left side of my bed and was just about to sit on it.

'Would you be able to sit on the other side of me, Carina?'

'Em, well I'm not sure I should.'

'Please, looking towards my left is hard for me to do. My neck's sore and it hurts my head.'

'Kieran will kill me. He said the doctor wants everything to be done from your left. We've to sit here so you'll use your muscles on the left. "Left-sided neglect" or something like that, he said.'

'OK then.'

'How are you?'

'It's hard-going, Carina. I'm in so much pain all the time and my son – my baby isn't with me,' I said starting to cry. 'Carina, what's Dylan like?'

'Oh he's just so beautiful. But of course we all knew he would be with parents like you and Kieran.'

I smiled at the compliment.

'What does he do when you're minding him?'

'The times he's with me, he sleeps and when he wakes, he smiles wanting to be fed. Imagine! Your child gurgles when he's hungry and every other child screams the house down.'

'Bring him up to the hospital the next time you're here.'

I watched Carina as she started to shuffle on the chair.

'Kim, you probably don't remember, but we're returning home a few days after the final Mug-Out party.'

How can you do this to me when I need you to stay? I need your help. I've so many things on my mind. You're my friend and I need to talk to you.

'He'll leave me.'

'Who?'

'Kieran. He won't stay with a wife who can't walk. He'll take Dylan and go.'

110

'Are you completely crazy?' Carina said, taking a tissue from her handbag and handing it to me. 'You and Kieran have the tightest bond I've ever seen in a relationship, everyone says so. If the two of you can't last the pace, then there's little hope for the rest of us. Don't be so ridiculous.'

'But Kieran won't want to live with this,' I said, pointing at my disabled body.

'Stop now,' she said firmly. 'You know that's not going to happen. I used to watch you during the year all loved up in each other's company. Kieran's lucky to have you.'

Then changing the subject, she said, 'It's so hot in the house. Our air conditioning isn't working and I'm trying to pack up everything. It's a nightmare. Remember we brought over too much stuff, well now I'm bringing home too much.'

'When are you going?'

'The Mug-Out is on tonight and then we're leaving Monday.'

'What?' I couldn't believe it. 'The Mug-Out tonight?'

She nodded.

'I wish I was able to go,' I said, feeling a loss that I wouldn't be part of the finale. The final curtain of the tour was being lowered and I wouldn't be there.

'We're not sure if it will go ahead or not. No one feels like celebrating when you're so sick.'

Her voice quivered. It was her turn to show emotion. She leant over and we hugged.

Lost in her embrace, I felt a hand on my back

'Hi Carina,' Kieran said, lifting his hand from me. 'Thanks for staying with Kim.'

'She's going home in a few days' time.'

'I know we'll miss you. You have helped me so much. I don't know what I would have done without you. You and (our friend) Ann, got no sleep the night you came over to help me and then you took Dylan for the following day and a half. You both shopped, cooked and minded me and our families: we will be forever in your debt, thank you.'

A flashback of Carina bending over me made me wonder if I was beginning to remember something from the actual night I became ill.

'It was nothing. I only wish I wasn't going home before you're better Kim. But it won't be long before you're up and about. You'll be the most glamorous mother tottering around in your high-heels and designer baby-bag. Look I'd better go. I won't say goodbye because we'll meet up loads when you're back in Ballina. Take care.'

She scurried out of the ward. I watched her take a tissue from her bag and bring it up to her face.

And without turning back she was gone.

'Carina was truly brilliant. They all are,' Kieran said, wiping my tears with the tissue she'd left on my bed.

'The Mug-Out is on tonight, isn't it?'

'Yeah, I've told the contingent I'm not going.'

'Of course you're going. You designed the slideshow.'

'No, it wouldn't be right.'

'What wouldn't be right?'

'I wouldn't feel right being there when you're in hospital.'

'Please go Kieran. Mum will be here with me.'

'She's too tired Kim to stay with you all night. I'm not going to the Mug-Out and that's final. But what I might do, if it's OK, is take your Mum out tomorrow night for our wedding anniversaries.'

'Yes that's a good idea.'

Exactly a year ago Mum and I had gone out for lunch to celebrate our joint wedding anniversaries. Kieran wasn't with us because he had left Ireland to go to Cyprus. Now he was celebrating my parents' 45th wedding anniversary and our 12th without me.

'Sinéad said she'll come in to stay with you,' Kieran explained.

'She's so good. I'll look forward to her company.'

'You know, it won't be the same without you.'

'You don't say,' I said sarcastically, thinking that a mother-in-law and a son-in-law going out to dinner was the least romantic way a man and woman could celebrate their wedding anniversaries.

'I want to bring your Mum out as a kind of thank you.'

I nodded, appreciating his thoughtful gesture.

He stood up from the bed and looked down at me.

'Come on. It's time for you to see the rest of the hospital. Let's go for a walk.'

I looked at him.

'But we tried it yesterday and I couldn't even get into the wheelchair.'

He was determined. He held me under the arms and manoeuvred me to the side of the bed.

'We'll try this again and if it doesn't work and you're not able to sit up, we can try again tomorrow.'

'It would be nice to get out of here for a while and see what's going on outside of my ward.'

Why is this happening to me? I'm missing my son.

'I'm going to get a wheelchair and we'll go and get ice-cream.'

'Help! Come back! I'm falling,' I roared after him.

Kieran caught me just as I was toppling over the side of the bed. I hadn't sat up straight for a long time and with the loss of some functioning core muscles, I hadn't the strength to hold myself up.

Sometime later we were ready to go. I was in the wheelchair but I kept slumping over on my left side. Kieran had an idea.

'I'll get a bed sheet and tie it around you so you won't fall on your side.'

When I was strapped securely into the wheelchair, we started to exit the ward.

'Kim, your arm is going to catch in the wheel. Put it back on your lap where I placed it a minute ago.'

I brought my right hand across my body and I lifted my left arm back onto my knee as instructed.

'Kim, you're falling out, sit back up straight.'

'Oh, I didn't know.'

A few feet later.

'Kieran, I'm going to be sick.'

'That's OK, we'll turn around.'

'No, I'll be fine. I'm just a bit dizzy. Don't push too fast.'

There was a whole new world outside. The Nurses' Station was directly opposite the door of the ward, and from behind the counter the matron lifted her head briefly.

'It's good to see you up, enjoy your walk.'

The hospital was a maze of corridors with wards of various sizes feeding the main thoroughfare. Cypriot cleanliness prevailed in this hospital as it had when I'd given birth in the hospital in Larnaca.

Abruptly Kieran brought the wheelchair to a halt. An attractive Cypriot woman in her early-fifties approached us. She smiled at me, took my hand and gave it a little squeeze.

'Nice,' she said, looking blankly into my eyes.

'How's your husband?' Kieran asked.

'The same.'

'I'm sorry.'

Kieran started to push me towards the lift and I smiled a goodbye at her, not knowing who she was.

Kieran was quiet and we didn't speak for a while until we were eating ice-cream in the rather pathetic-looking coffee shop at the main entrance of the hospital.

'Who's that woman?' I asked.

'Her husband had a brain haemorrhage too but hasn't been conscious for fourteen days. I got talking to her outside ICU when you and her husband were both fighting for your lives. You've survived but unfortunately it's not looking good for him.'

I'd a brain haemorrhage, a brain haemorrhage! Oh my God, a brain haemorrhage! It sounds bad – anything to do with the

115

head isn't good. What's a brain haemorrhage? I never met anyone who had a brain haemorrhage before.

'What happened to me?'

'You want to know from the start?'

'I remember going to bed that night and waking up screaming – I thought my bones were bursting through my skin and my arm was coming out of its socket. Kieran, I screamed and screamed for you. You didn't hear me.'

Kieran's account

I DID hear you, and I came running into the bedroom. You were hysterical and hallucinating. Carina and I brought you to the maternity hospital in Larnaca.

Dr Kassinis phoned a neurologist and radiologist. You were brought for a MRI scan by these men who had been woken from their beds. Your eyes were open but you weren't able to talk, except for the odd monosyllable which didn't make any sense. I sat on a chair in the corridor and began to process what was happening. I spoke to an inner spirit: some would call it God. I was asking this spirit to please allow my wife to just be food poisoned – she'd be better soon.

Suddenly, the doors of the x-ray room opened. You seemed OK. I looked up at Dr Kassinis.

'What's happening to Kim?'

His answer brought my world crashing down into a surreal place.

'Kim is having a brain haemorrhage.'

I know it was a silly question, but I asked him if it was serious. Do you remember we used to ask him this question when you were pregnant?

He just said, 'This is very serious. The next 72 hours are critical. Look at the MRI scan.'

Even to the untrained eye, it looked frightening. The haemorrhage was massive.

'We will call an ambulance and get her to Nicosia hospital. Now I will take out her stitches from the Caesarean section.'

He returned to the Nurses' Station and started to make more phone calls.

I checked on you and you were staring into oblivion. You then started to convulse. The panic of the nurses and the response of the doctors told me it was time to phone your Mum, whilst you were still alive.

I'd heard enough for the moment. I'd ask Mum later when she'd come to visit.

Mum's account

ON July 24 their beautiful baby was born and when Kieran and Kim rang to say they had a little boy called Dylan, I cried all day with happiness.

It was the happiest day of my life. I wanted to be over with Kim, to give her the biggest hug and let her know how much I loved her.

On July 31, disaster struck. In the middle of the night the phone rang. As I was reaching for the receiver, I had a feeling it was Kieran but I was not prepared for what he had to tell me. Kim had had a brain haemorrhage and she was paralysed down her left side.

All of the sudden my whole world fell apart. Kim was lying in hospital in Nicosia and I was in Dublin, not knowing whether she would live or die. My daughter, Ann, insisted she would come with me to Cyprus so she could mind Dylan while I was with Kim and vice versa.

We arrived in Larnaca that night to be met by two of Kieran's colleagues. The hospital in Nicosia was closed to visitors for the night so we went to Kieran and Kim's house and found our little grandson; he was so beautiful and so good. He was only one week old, but I loved him from the first moment I saw him.

The next morning, Ann and I went into the hospital. I went into ICU to see Kim, not knowing how I was going to find her. She was lying there with her eyes rolling in her head, but when I said, 'Kim, I'm here,' she answered, 'Hi Mum,' which was a huge relief to me. I don't know how long I sat with her, but it was so good to be beside her. She was quite calm and we had been told not to let her talk, just to rest.

The next day I went back to the hospital. When I arrived into Kim, I knew she was much worse than the day before and I got really upset. On two occasions when I was with her, the alarm bells she was wired to went off. I phoned my husband and Carla and said they had better come over as our youngest daughter had got worse.

Kieran and I were called in to talk to the doctors. Kieran took my hand as we really felt that we had lost our Kim. No words can describe the pain we were both going through at that time.

'Your wife is alive but seriously ill,' the neurosurgeon explained. 'We need to remove the stale blood in her brain as she could die from septicaemia, but we need your consent to do the operation.'

'What are her chances of survival?' Kieran asked him.

'About 50/50 and even if she survives I don't know what damage the haemorrhage will have done and how she will be left. Do you want time to think about it?'

'Yes.'

'You have twenty minutes.'

It was like a very bad dream, as if it wasn't really happening to us, and yet it was.

Kieran phoned a radiologist friend of his in Dublin for advice and a short while later our decision was made – within five minutes Kim was taken down to theatre.

We prayed like we never prayed before. The waiting was awful.

After two hours a doctor came towards us. He was looking our way but I focused my eyes on the floor lest I recognised failure in his eyes.

'The operation was successful. We were able to remove the haematoma.'

Kieran and I smiled at each other. Things were looking up.

The next morning Kim was still in ICU. She was conscious and was able to whisper and communicate with us – which was so wonderful. It was so emotional for us to know she was alive and responding.

From then on the doctors told us it would be a very slow progress, but hopefully she would recover.

She went through a very tough time in hospital for the next month. I stayed with Kim and Dylan for the month of August. Both of them, mother and son, needed round the clock care.

On the few occasions we brought Dylan in to see Kim, she got very upset when she'd see her baby because she wasn't there for him, and at other times she wasn't well enough for him. I found it very difficult to watch my daughter's grief. I was helpless. She was trying to come to terms with her disability, her illness and her absent son. It was heart-breaking to see her in such distress and me not being able to do anything to relieve her pain.

Then suddenly, the hospital said she was fit to go home at the end of August, so in one day we had to move house from Pyla to Nicosia. Once again the Gardaí turned up trumps and under Kieran's guidance they got everything moved from one house to the other in a few hours.

Leaving hospital

DUE to the long delay waiting for a doctor to discharge me from the hospital, it was dusk by the time we left to go into Nicosia city centre. Kieran had been rushing around the hospital all day looking for surgeons and hadn't eaten since early that morning. He was hungry and needed to fill the hungry void in his stomach, so we drove towards McDonald's on the way to our new house.

The glare of car headlights and the city noise were making me queasy. I hadn't been outside for nearly a month and the street and neon lights were strange and unnerving.

Exhaustion and a need to lie down to ease the pain in the muscles in my bottom were foremost on my mind but I'd to respect Kieran's need for sustenance.

The girl at the window in the Drive-Thru handed Kieran his Big Mac Meal. He pulled over and started to eat. I was nauseous as I smelled the onions and gherkins from the oversized burger.

'There you go, take it,' he said, rummaging in the paper bag and taking out a cheese burger which he had secretly bought for me.

'No thanks.'

'You haven't eaten all day.'

'No.'

I was defiant and I made it very clear I was on a diet of roughage and nothing else. I was obsessed by my bowel movements and wouldn't allow any saturated fats or carbohydrates past my mouth.

'Are you finished? I really need to get to the British Army house and lie down,' I asked meekly.

'Just give me a minute, Kim. It's been a tough day for me too!' he said, exasperated. 'We're all doing our best for you. We'll get to the UNPA when I'm ready.'

I bowed my head.

After hearing of our plight, the Britcon (British Army Contingent), whose headquarters was in the UNPA, had been very kind and had offered Kieran one of their vacant, married family quarters. These houses were for British officers and their families when they were based in Cyprus, but the Britcon had bypassed their rules and given three Irish citizens a home.

In preparation for me moving into the house, modifications had to be made to both the exterior and interior of the house. A ramp was built at the front door. Handrails had been screwed into the wall in the bathroom, a cot and extra beds were placed in the bedrooms for us. Their maintenance staff was available to us whenever we needed them. No task was too big.

People had been so accommodating – I had no right to ask for anything from anyone. I'd wait until Kieran's chips were finished.

But Kieran didn't finish his meal at the Drive-Thru. He knew I wasn't one to over-exaggerate an ailment so instead he switched on the engine and started to drive. He was still dipping his hand into the paper bag and eating his skinny chips when we arrived into the maze of houses in the UNPA.

I looked out the car window and saw some old detached bungalows. Some of the houses were blatantly unoccupied with overgrown gardens. Other houses had life, were well-kept and had toys strewn on the front lawns. The Patch, as it was known, was where British families were living military lives.

'This is ours,' Kieran said, pointing to a bungalow on my right.

There were lights on in the house and street lights shone on the neglected scorched grass in the front garden which was surrounded by a small, white picket-fence. My husband helped me from the car and we headed towards the front door.

'We're here!' Kieran shouted, lifting me through the front door and putting me back into my wheelchair.

Being carried over a threshold used to have a different meaning for me. It was for newly married couples blissful with their lives mapped out in front of them. My carefully mapped-out life had gone off course.

My sister, Carla, had returned to Cyprus and was walking around the sitting-room winding a baby. She stroked the baby's back gently and milk spewed over her shoulder and trickled down her back.

She stopped and smiled at me, 'Hi Kim. It's so good to see you.'

'Hi Carla. Thanks so much for coming over to help us. I really appreciate it.'

I looked around the large rectangular room. A thin grey carpet was on the floor, a blue couch and two matching armchairs were placed opposite each other. The house was old but the furnishings were clean and relatively new. A dining-table was at one end of the room and the kitchen and pantry appeared to be off the dining area.

Suddenly startled, I looked back at Carla. I froze. She was stroking *my baby*! It had seemed so natural to see her as a mother, that momentarily I had forgotten the baby was mine.

My stomach retched.

It should be me holding him, but instead of me winding my five-week-old baby, Kieran was helping me on to the small couch. I couldn't sit, the pain was too much for me so I asked to be put lying on my back. Dylan started to cry.

'Maybe Carla, you should take Dylan out of the room to give Kim some time to rest?' Mum asked.

'No!' I screeched, 'Don't. He's mine. I want to hold him!'

Kieran stepped forward and looking at Mum and Carla, he said, 'I'll take him. Would you mind giving Kim and me some time alone?'

My mother and sister scampered out the sitting room door.

Kieran placed Dylan on my chest and I studied his features closely. He had changed considerably from the last time I'd seen him. The most recent baby photos which my thoughtful friend, Sandra, had stuck around my hospital bed were very different to the little person lying on me. A baby's unique scent and gurgling sounds can't be caught on camera.

'Aren't you just gorgeous my little baby? I've come home. I'm so sorry I left you. I didn't want to but I'm back now. I love you and promise I'll make it up to you. Each day I was in hospital, Daddy told me all about you.'

Kieran was leaning over cuddling the two of us and our tears fell in rivers onto Dylan's pyjamas. My shoulders were heaving as I sobbed and I tried to hold Dylan in my right arm but I felt him slipping out of my grasp.

'Will I take him?'

I let go and Kieran protectively lifted Dylan up into his arms. Kieran had always been a natural with babies. He was ten-years-old when his youngest sibling was born, and in a family of ten, he had to learn how to take care of his baby brother. His mother was extremely demonstrative with children so he'd an excellent role model to learn from.

I watched Kieran bounce Dylan on his lap. Pictures of our house in Pyla began to flash in and out of my head. I didn't know why we were now living in land-locked Nicosia when we had spent a whole year living in bliss by the coast. I wanted to return to my old life. I wanted everything back the way it was.

Bring me home. Bring me back home.

Kieran sensed my apprehension and explained delicately, 'There are stairs in our house in Pyla. I wouldn't be able to carry you up them. The physiotherapists are here in Nicosia and it makes more sense to live in a bungalow near the physiotherapy clinic.'

It wasn't about the house, in truth I didn't mind where I was living. I just wanted to go back in time. But for the moment I'd go with it. If he thought living in the capital city was our best option, then he was probably right. I hadn't made any essential decisions for a while and I was reliant on others to decide what was best for me.

I started to yawn, and struggling in pain, I said, 'Will you ask Carla to put me to bed?'

Kieran went off to find her and she returned to the sitting room.

'I'll help you into your chair and bring you down the corridor to your room,' she said.

The vast bedroom had a single and a double bed side-by-side. The beds were immaculately dressed in the way Mum always dressed beds. The duvet cover had pressed iron-lines down the centre and the top pillow was balancing perfectly, almost floating on the bottom pillow. My toiletries and jewellery filled a dressing table, but I had no need for any of these frivolities for the moment, and I barred them from my mind.

Carla wheeled me towards the single bed, helped me out of the chair and placed me on the side of the bed. As she undressed me, I looked down at my withered body which was still showing the after-effects of child birth. Old scabs on my nipples were crusted over. The indented C-section incision pulled my skin tightly across my lower abdomen and it displayed a dry coating of blood which was blistering from the stitched skin.

The rest of my body appeared normal and I was happy I had no stretch marks or remaining baby fat. In a few weeks I'd be back in my bikini on the beach, holidaying with my new family.

I don't understand what all the fuss is about trying to shift baby weight.

I didn't realise I had lost five stone in the five weeks following Dylan's birth (half of which was baby-related).

I closed my eyes and Carla carefully manoeuvred my left arm into my nightie, then my right, before pulling the cool nightdress over my head. She had trained as an occupational therapist and her nurturing way made me feel safe. She helped me to lie down and tried to ease the crushing pain in my bottom by placing two red IKEA cushions under the left side of my lower body where the muscles were beginning to wilt from lack of use.

I had bought these cushions when we were living in Pyla to add colour to the living-room. They had lasted the year, hadn't bleached in the sun and still looked as good as new. When I was pregnant, I had used the largest one to support my back when I was slouched on the couch watching DVDs. The other cushion was just as effective: I'd placed it on a little coffee table to rest my swollen ankles.

Now these simple cushions felt even more comforting, albeit in a different way. It was nice to have something familiar and soft from our other house.

My eyes started to close. Kieran entered the room.

'I've to give you this medication,' he said, meticulously counting tablets from various bottles.

He read the dosages twice, placed a glass of water in my hand and put one tablet after the next into my mouth. I wasn't quite sure what the tablets were for but he seemed to know what he was doing. I obeyed and swallowed them down.

By next week I won't be taking any drugs. My body will be pure.

I drifted off to sleep.

Oh my God, I had a stroke!

I COULD see the morning rays of the sun sneaking through the closed white shutters and I was eager to get up. Kieran was stirring in the double bed. I wanted to shower and start my job of getting better.

We got up and he put me in the wheelchair. I was unable to keep my left leg safely resting on the foot-plate and my journey from the bedroom into the bathroom was hazardous. My leg banged against walls and doors. I hadn't much feeling in my left foot and bumps and bruises were part of the ritual.

There was no separate shower in the bathroom so Kieran placed me on the side of the bath. He stood behind and lifted me under my arms into a standing position. I held onto a handrail on the wall, he turned on the tap and water began to trickle down my bony body.

'Ah, it's too cold,' I said.

'OK, I'll add hot water.'

'Now it's too hot.'

Kieran apologised and got on with washing my hair using his own shower gel. Never in my life had I stooped so low as to use an all-in-one man's shampoo/gel but I wasn't in a position to ask him to use my luxurious shampoo and creamed-conditioner. From now on I was at the mercy of others and I knew there would be times I'd have to put some of my preferences and needs aside. People were kind to me and I couldn't keep asking them to do a chore in exactly the same way as I would have done it. It was time for me to relinquish some control and appreciate that, 'there are many ways to skin a cat.' But it was difficult giving part of me away and settling for what I didn't necessarily want.

'Oh God! What now?' I asked, when I saw clumps of hair beginning to block the drain.

My feet were unrecognisably covered in brown strands of long hair and little half-inch lengths. Both sides of my head were represented in that mesh.

'Get me out.'

'Why's your hair falling out?'

'I don't know!' I exclaimed, before the truth dawned on me. 'It must be from after having Dylan. Carina had said it might happen, women can lose hair following the birth of a baby.'

He cuddled me.

'Don't worry then. It's normal.'

He dried my body with one of my designer bath-towels, which I bought in boom times before we'd left for Cyprus. Following a year's constant use, this overly-expensive towel had remained soft and fluffy and it felt nice against my skin. He threw the towel over my head and I smiled at his little gesture of humour.

Even though only half of my head was covered in hair (which was beginning to fall out) there was still an awful lot of it. I had very thick hair and in those early September temperatures, the heat was already building up behind my neck and shoulders and I was beginning to sweat.

'Do you think I'll be able to do a comb-over like Uncle Henry?' I asked, flicking the hair across my head onto the right side and nearly blinding myself in the process.

'Come here you. Let me sort you out. Look at the state of you!'

I found his perverse comment funny.

'Understatement of the year!'

'I didn't mean it like that, Kim. I'm sorry.'

'No, it's hilarious!'

I started to laugh but soon the laughter turned to uncontrollable crying.

Kieran bent down and hugged me tightly.

'We'll get through this. I love you. Come on, let's get dressed and have something to eat.'

The dining room table was set for breakfast but all I wanted was a cup of tea. Food was my enemy and I was afraid to allow anything to clog up my digestive system.

'Kim you need to build up your energy. You've a long day in front of you,' my mother explained.

'I'll have a small bowl of bran later.'

'You have to eat, Kim. Promise me you'll eat when I go home.'

Mum was returning to Ireland that day and I was both heart-broken and relieved she was going. She was physically and emotionally exhausted. She needed to get home to recuperate and be minded by her ever-supporting husband.

She was close to collapsing and was trying to assimilate all that was happening to her daughter.

Mum's brother had died the previous week and she had yet to offer her condolences to his family or begin to grieve his passing.

'Mum, go home,' I'd said to her in the hospital when she'd told me her eldest sibling had died.

'I can't leave you.'

'But he's your brother.'

'Hush now, his family understands why I won't be at the funeral. You're my little girl and you're my priority at the moment.'

Her needs were on hold until she returned to the bosom of her loved ones. A month of turmoil was taking its toll on her and I was afraid for her health.

Little cries coming from the Moses basket halted our conversation. My tiny infant was looking for his breakfast and a bottle needed to be made. Mum went into the kitchen, returned and placed the bottle of milk on the table. She carefully lifted Dylan out and brought him over to me.

Dylan was wearing one of the white babygros I had bought in Mothercare a month prior to his birth. It was sleeveless, short-legged and there was a motif on the front, saying 'Mummy's Boy.' She handed him to me and helped me hold him on my knee. I stroked his perfect little nose and looked into his eyes.

'I'm your Mummy.'

He looked away.

I looked at my Mum's face.

'He doesn't know who I am. I'm a stranger to him. When other mothers are getting to know their babies I was fighting for my life. I've only spent a few hours with him since my brain haemorrhage.'

My second set of tears of the morning fell onto his forehead and they kept falling until he was removed from my arms. I turned my head to the side.

'What's up?' Kieran asked, entering the dining room with the keys of the car in his hand.

'He doesn't know me,' I kept saying. 'My baby doesn't know who I am.'

'He does. You're home now and he'll get to know his Mummy very soon. OK? We'd better get going.'

I nodded and allowed myself be ushered to the car to start my first day of intensive physiotherapy. Kieran helped me into the front passenger seat, ensuring my four limbs were inside before shutting the door. We were two kilometres from the city centre and as the sun rose over Nicosia, I sat in the car in a daze.

'Tell me five good things.'

This had been our ritual since I was in hospital. I had to list five positive things in my life at that particular time. I had come up with the idea which was supposed to perk me up for a while.

'Number 1 is Dylan. Number 2 is you. Number 3 is my son having a mother. Number 4 is my voice and sight returning and Number 5 is my family.'

My answers were becoming repetitive. At that time I wasn't able to find joy in sunsets, material things, music or conversations.

As I looked through the windscreen at the office blocks, restaurants and shops in Nicosia, I watched the urgency of men and women weaving through traffic trying to cross the road. City-women were stylish, and many weeks ago I would have admired their leather handbags, trendy clothes and designer sunglasses. Now I was in a stupor and couldn't understand how their lives were continuing normally when mine wasn't.

Can't you tell I'm suffering?

The car came to a halt – we had arrived at the old-folks' home where the physiotherapists who specialised in injuries like mine, were working. The new three-storey building stood at the side of the road and it cast a shadow over us. Kieran followed a sign which was directing us from the street into a dark basement car park.

When Kieran was reversing the car into a car park space, I looked around the basement. Directly to the side of the entrance to the physiotherapy clinic, there were trolleys stacked high with sheets, ready to go to a laundry. Two Zimmer-frames and a disused wheelchair with a broken wheel were strewn across a car park space close to the clinic's access point. Kieran helped me from the car, wheeled me through the obstacles and we entered the door.

The glare of halogen lighting brightly lit the clinic and the air conditioning made it feel cool. A long corridor focused my eyes straight ahead and I could see the door of a gym towards the end of the passageway. There were rooms off the corridor and professional young men and women in tracksuits flitted from room to room.

'I'll go and find the manager,' Kieran said, leaving me on the corridor.

I felt alone and out of my depth in this new environment. Up until then, I hadn't got to know the real Cyprus or Cypriot people. Our lives had been based around tourist areas and we had been blanketed by English-speaking internationals. This was the first time for me to experience ordinary Cypriot life.

Three people were seated beside me on the corridor. My presence was obviously breaking their monotony, and as they looked my way, I felt exposed and vulnerable.

Suddenly, my nose started to twitch.

A kitchen door must have just opened allowing a smell to waft towards me. It was the comforting aroma of bread baking in the oven: the unmistakable smell I used to get when I'd come home after school when I was a child and find warm scones on the kitchen table. I smiled.

Perhaps I'll be OK here.

Kieran returned with a woman by his side.

'This is Andry. She and her husband will be working with you over the next few months.'

'Hi Keem, you are very welcome,' she said, offering me a warm smile.

I love the way Cypriots pronounce my name.

Andry, my physiotherapist, was a little different to some of the women I witnessed posing up and down the promenade in Larnaca or strutting on Nissi beach in Agia Napa. She wasn't at all self-absorbed. Instead, she was friendly, smiley, and welcoming. Her English was good and she chatted to me briefly, before introducing me to her physiotherapist-husband, Kostas.

'Hello Keem, you are welcome.'

'Hello.'

'Come, I will show you some of the clinic.'

Kostas was wearing blue scrubs, similar to the green scrubs I had seen the doctors wear in the hospital, and even though the air conditioning was on, he had sweat on his brow. He pushed me towards the gym in the end room where old men and women were engaged in various exercises. There were hand-rotation bikes, treadmills, weights and other equipment. Two patients were sitting at exercise bikes, peddling, trying to coerce the muscles in their weak legs to strengthen.

They're all so old. I've been duped. I shouldn't be here.

'When you have stroke?' an elderly woman asked me in broken English.

'I didn't have a stroke. I had a brain haemorrhage.'

'Yes, you stroke.'

I don't know what she means. The word stroke has nothing to do with my brain haemorrhage. Old people have strokes.

I thought perhaps the word was lost in translation and asked for clarification from Kostas.

'Why did that woman say I'd a stroke?'

'Of course you had, that's why you here in my clinic. We specialises with stroke.'

'But, but, I was told I'd a brain haemorrhage.'

'Yes, you had a haemorrhagic stroke. You bleed in your brain; you had a stroke.'

I was appalled.

I never knew a brain haemorrhage is the same as a stroke.

I asked my family never to use the term *stroke* – a brain haemorrhage was much more acceptable in my eyes. People of any age could have brain haemorrhages but people of my age didn't have strokes. I didn't want to hear the word associated with my illness as I felt ashamed. I put this diagnostic word to the back of my mind, never to be used again. I hoped no one in Ireland would ever find out I'd had a stroke.

What have I done to myself to cause a stroke? Everyone will talk about me behind my back. They'd nod in a knowing way as if to say it was inevitable – she wasn't fit, she'd a sweet tooth, she was too old to get pregnant... she deserved it.

Kostas continued to show me around the clinic. We stopped in a room, where a black plinth was pushed against a wall.

'I need to strap you onto the plinth and then I've a remote-control to lift the bed up,' Kostas said to me.

He asked me to lie down on my back and he secured me in place with large black straps. The bed started to tilt upwards and I felt nauseous at the sensation of the bed moving.

The twenty minutes I was strapped to the vertically-positioned plinth, gave me time to think. I hadn't stood for such a long time and my body and digestive system were re-experiencing this otherwise normal everyday activity. As the dizziness subsided, I adjusted my eyes to my surroundings.

Straight ahead of me stood a large ceiling-to-floor mirror.

I was startled by what I saw. I knew half of my head had been shaved a month previous, but I hadn't seen the result. My hair was emulating my body. One half was appealing and the other half was despicable.

What happened to me? Where have I gone? Who's this decrepit woman looking back at me from the mirror? I want my body back again. I want my baby.

'Kieran, I need to get it cut,' I said to him, when he came into the room later and stared at me in my Hannibal Lecter position.

'What cut?'

'My hair. It's too long on this side, it needs to come off. I look ridiculous.'

'Are you sure you want to?'

'I haven't any choice.'

'If you're sure about it, we can go on the way home.'

Is this really happening to me? Of all the people in the world, why me?

A function in the Ambassador's residence

THE hairdresser's was painted in a warm green colour and was accessorised with cream lilies in ornate vases. The scent from the flowers was being overpowered by a strong smell of lemon coming from an oil-burner resting on the reception-desk. Walnut panelling framed large mirrors and red and cream leather chairs were pushed under opaque glass shelves. Hairdryers and hair products were neatly stored to the right of the mirrors.

Five young hairdressers in skimpy tops, skinny jeans or flowing skirts were busy chatting to their clients. The sound of my wheelchair's footplates hitting off the steel legs of a chair, made them turn around to face me in unison – a vulnerable disabled woman who had arrived for a haircut. I was embarrassed being surrounded by such beauty. I too had been beautiful once.

'Would she like to sit here?' One of the girls awkwardly asked Kieran, pointing to a stylist's chair.

'I think it is easier for me to stay in the wheelchair,' I replied to the innocent hairdresser who must have been unsettled by my disability, and had directed her question towards Kieran.

My previous hairdressing experiences on the island had been very different. Rasmus' skill in Pyla's finest salon was extraordinary. I continuously had to remind him not to do 'big hair' and I was rarely totally pleased with his creation. Nonetheless, between the humidity and subsequent frizzy hair, I was a regular in the salon because he was able to bring the silkiness back into my heat-damaged tresses.

Now it was a different situation. A towel was placed around my shoulders and the cutting started. I kept my eyes on my feet so I wouldn't be able to look at myself in the mirror. I saw my curly locks lying on the floor. I didn't cry but I knew I would grieve this loss sometime in the future. Growing my hair long and its untimely crop, was something I had spent some of my early years battling. But I was now a grown-up and I'd many other problems – surely not being able to walk was worse than the loss of my hair?

'That looks good,' Kieran said when it was finished.

'Please don't. I don't want any comments about my hair until it has grown back to its normal length again.'

'OK, OK I won't. Anyway do you think you're up to going to this drinks party later this evening?'

'Why not?'

'You only just got out of hospital.'

'Yeah, I think I'd like to go.'

'Remember, there'll be a different group going tonight than there was the last time. The new contingent will be there.'

'I know but Sinéad and Sandra are going aren't they? I'm looking forward to meeting them again.'

Functions in the Ambassador's residence were always good and I wanted to attend. It was the eve of an international soccer match (Ireland v Cyprus) and the Ambassador was entertaining key FAI personnel, ex-pats and the new Irish Garda group.

I had always got dressed up when attending functions. This time was no different so I asked Carla to help me into my favourite dress. It was made from black cotton and had large white dots over the fabric. A red satin sash accentuated my tiny waist, and the netting in the underskirt helped it to flair out to just below my knee. I had worn the dress only once before and I had felt really good in it. Red shoes with white polka dots and seven-inch heels had finished the outfit perfectly. But there was no need to wear heels whilst sitting in a wheelchair, so regrettably my white Adidas runners and sport socks accessorised the dress.

Carla looked down at my feet.

'The runners are only a temporary measure and when you're walking again you'll be wearing those heels with this dress for many years to come. It'll just take a month or two and you'll be perfect once more.'

I nodded.

'I think it's time to go now. I'll help you into the car.'

Many were surprised I wanted to attend the function but I was eager to meet up with some friends who hadn't left the island yet.

Heads turned when Kieran, Carla and I arrived at the Irish Ambassador's residence. We ventured towards the crowd of people and I looked around demurely. This drinks party was similar to others: children were jumping in and out of the pool and the same delicacies were being passed around. The only difference was that I was unable to walk.

I heard a loud voice behind me and I looked around. One of Kieran's foreign colleagues was coming over to me.

Oh no, not you!

Although he was small in stature, he was portraying himself as a big man – the boss. He stood with a straight back and spoke down at me.

'I'm Agustín,' he said, as he extended his hand and squeezed my right hand.

'Yes.'

'You're very welcome.'

He lifted his gaze from me and I could see him scanning the crowd searching for another worthy cause.

I was dumbfounded and insulted by his introduction. I had met Agistín many times before – I'd even cooked dinner for him in our house. I was astounded he thought I wouldn't recognise him.

Perhaps it was he who didn't recognise me.

'Asshole!' I muttered to Carla, turning my head away from this man's smiling face.

'Don't worry about eejits like him, you're doing great,' she whispered back.

Agustín was now speaking to a FAI official about the upcoming soccer match.

'Come on over here and we'll meet some of the new contingent,' Kieran said to Carla and me, breaking us away from Agustín.

I was nervous going through the crowded patio-area. People were looking down at me in sympathy, smiling and then glancing away.

'Sinéad,' I said when she approached and got down on her honkers to be at my height. 'Thank God you're here. This is harder than I thought it would be.'

'You're doing brilliantly. Everyone has so much admiration for you and they want the very best for you. Let me know who you want to chat to and I'll bring them over.'

'Sandra, where's Sandra?' I asked.

I needed to see her and talk to her. She was leaving the island to return to Ireland the next day and I wanted to be with her for the last time.

Feeling a tightening of my hand, I looked up to see Sandra squeezing my fingers and smiling kindly.

'Hi Kim, I saw Mister-not-so-subtle talking to you. I hope he was nice.'

'Mm, what do you think?' I mumbled, still feeling somewhat hurt by my encounter with him. 'What time is your flight booked for? I wish I was going with you.'

'Tomorrow at seven. It's so hard leaving you. I'm sorry things turned out the way they did.'

All of a sudden Sandra stumbled. I looked at the culprit who was elbowing her out of the way.

'Hi, I'm Dolores,' an executive-looking woman said, in a high-pitched voice.

'Oh?'

She bent down and shook my hand. I felt her long red-painted talons digging into my palm. Her large bosom, which was toppling out of a white work shirt, was partially brushing intrusively against my nose. Her perfume wasn't masking the smell of gin either. Nothing about this woman was subtle.

'Oh?' I repeated.

'It was terrible what happened to you. It didn't look good for you for a while. We were so worried. Aren't you looking great?'

She was smiling at me as though we knew one another. I nodded slowly, hoping she'd leave.

Her energy was over-powering and her squeaky voice wasn't doing anything for me to feel confidence in her. I looked around for assistance but Sandra was now chatting to Sinéad, and they were oblivious to the intensity of this stranger from whom I was unable to escape. But she wasn't finished yet.

'I suggested that Dylan get an emergency passport when we thought you would be air-ambulanced back to Ireland. I was the one who realised a passport needed to be done straight away.'

I had no idea who she was and why she felt the need to pounce on me when I was facing into an already emotionally-charged situation. The organisation of an emergency passport was news to me and I was unprepared for this inappropriate personal information being publicly bandied around.

What had been going on in the background when I was in hospital? People were organising things I wasn't even aware of. Kieran never told me I might have been flown home. What else was discussed without my knowledge?

146

'That's great,' Kieran said sarcastically, pulling me away from Dolores so he could explain to me what she meant.

I could tell he was cross at her insensitively.

'I don't know who the hell she is. She kept appearing in the hospital. I don't even know her nationality. But yes, she's right, we didn't know what the medical system was like here and thought we'd to get you to Ireland as soon as possible. In the end, there was no need: you got fantastic care here and Irish diplomats have been hugely accommodating during this time. I'm really grateful to them.

'Sorry I didn't intercept that lunatic earlier. A function is no place for her to discuss these matters.'

Imagine a week-old baby getting a passport. Surely it would have been dangerous for him to fly when he was so young. My poor baby.

I was unable to stay at the party for very long as the pain in my muscles were beginning to cause me distress and we decided to leave.

'Carla, where's Sandra? I need to say goodbye. Where is she?'

I was frantic; where was she?

'Here she is!'

Kieran was strolling up behind us, chatting to Sandra. I breathed a sigh of relief.

'Sandra, there you are!'

'Kim, I'll see you soon when you get back to Ireland,' she uttered, bending down and giving me a hug.

'Goodbye, my great friend.'

147

'You're doing great and you'll be better very soon.'

'I know.'

'It's been both a brilliant and a tough time for you this year, but you have Dylan.'

'I know.'

We hugged and wiped the tears from each other's eyes. As I nuzzled my face into her hair, I knew I'd never forget her scent. I'd never forget her.

She turned, looked back, waved and got into her car.

Don't go! Don't leave me here. Everyone is leaving us behind. Carina and Ann have gone. Sinéad is the only one left. Don't go.

But a week later in mid-September, Sinéad and her husband called up to our house in the UNPA to see Kieran and me. My heart dropped. The inevitable was happening.

'You're going back, aren't you?' I pronounced.

'Yes, the flight's tonight.'

'You're lucky, you know that, don't you?'

'Yes I am, but you're lucky to have Dylan.'

'I am extremely lucky to have him. He's my reason for living.'

'Let's go for a walk,' she suggested.

'Yeah, that's a good idea. Can you get the baby-sling and put Dylan in it so he can sit on my lap?'

Sinéad had never been afraid of my paralysed side and was quite capable of helping Dylan and me in and out of the wheelchair. She placed Dylan in the sling which she wrapped around my body, and gently put him on my lap.

As we ambled through clusters of houses in the British enclave, we reminisced and chortled at events which had happened throughout the year. She gave me so much hope that Kieran, Dylan and I would be OK again and things would work out.

Their visit to our house was poignant. It meant Kieran and I were going to be on our own. There was no one left. If there is a word stronger than desertion, I would have used it that day to describe how I felt watching the last of our contingent-friends leave to return to their old lives in Ireland.

Many months before, on Nissi beach, Sinéad, Sandra and I had looked for ways to stay on in Cyprus. It seemed as though I was the only one who was given that opportunity, but I hadn't asked for it like this.

Depression was beginning to set in.

The stages of grief

ALTHOUGH my friends had all gone, I still stayed in contact with them. They sent words of encouragement in texts every day, helping me navigate through my loss. My close friends from home phoned and texted too – each contact made, became a little thread of hope I could hold onto. I needed them to hear and feel my raw pain, and I needed their words of comfort. I kept hoping someone somewhere could help me deal with my emotional torment. I had lost half my body at the most important time of my life. I'd never worried about being a good mother, but now I was tormented.

How can I be the mother I thought I'd be when I'm reliant on others to help? I'm not independent, I'm dependent. I'm not showing Dylan off to people, they're showing him to me.

Night times got significantly worse. I went to sleep quickly enough but I could be awake from 4 a.m. Horrendous thoughts came in and out of my head. Suicide was one recurring theme which kept my mind occupied. I knew deep down I'd never self-harm: I'd a baby and a husband whom I desperately cherished and I'd never put them through the trauma of believing I didn't love them enough to stay alive. But I was distraught and I wanted out of the life I was living.

I wondered was I going mad because I'd never experienced such depths of despair before. Whilst I planned ways to take my life, I knew it was only my way of describing the extent of my pain; besides my little boy was entitled to a mother.

'What's going on?' Ann, my sister, asked when she was driving me to an osteopath one evening.

'I feel suicidal.'

'Can you tell me about it?'

I broke down and blurted out my private thoughts. She listened to me carefully and she asked me to tell her my suicide intent. I spoke of over-dosing and toppling over a nearby cliff. Once the words were out, they lost power and I was able to acknowledge the futility of my plan.

'But I can't understand the level of sadness I'm experiencing. I can't believe I've had a brain haemorrhage.'

'Kim, you're grieving the loss of the person you were, the person you thought you'd be and the plans which never came true.'

I didn't say anything as I pondered over her words.

'I never thought about it that way. It makes sense now. I'm going through the stages of grief. I haven't lost my mind. This is what grief feels like.'

'Can you remember the stages?' she asked.

'Denial, anger, bargaining and depression,' I said without taking a breath. 'I can't remember any more. Can you?'

'Acceptance.'

It was only when Ann used the word 'grief,' everything became clear to me. I was going through the stages of grief. I knew the stages weren't linear. They would be felt at different times and I would drift in and out of each stage throughout the process. Understanding I was grieving lifted a load off my shoulder because I now knew I hadn't suddenly acquired an incurable mental illness.

'We're here,' I said, pointing to an apartment block. 'His clinic is just over there.'

Ann was bringing me to the osteopath who had successfully treated me when I had some back pain during my pregnancy and I'd faith he'd fix me now.

It was dark when we entered his clinic and sat in the waiting room. The wait was long and as the pain in my muscles increased, I shuffled uncomfortably in my seat. There were charts of the skeletal system on the wall. I searched each diagram to see if my weak muscles might be bone-related. I knew this wasn't it, but I yearned for the possibility the bones in my body could be manipulated back into position and I would be cured.

'Kim, come in,' he said, in a recognisable voice. 'Tell me what's wrong.'

Like a child, I looked pleadingly into Adonis's face. Wrinkles were etched around his eyes and his fair hair was mixed with some patches of grey strands which fifty years had produced. Sharp green eyes bore into mine.

'I'll help you onto the bed,' he said, a little dismissively.

Adonis lifted my legs and helped me to lie down. He was no longer at the same height as me and I was relieved I wasn't able to make eye contact with him anymore. I was getting different vibes from him. I couldn't understand why I felt rejected.

I told him everything that had happened but I could feel him looking at me in his I-told-you-so way.

Before Dylan was born, he'd voiced his opinion that I should insist on a natural birth; 'A C-section isn't good for you or the baby. That's the problem in Cyprus, the doctors do too many of them. You need to speak up for yourself.'

Foolishly, after my brain haemorrhage I questioned my reticence and stupidity for not following his advice. I took my decision to heart and started to believe that my brain haemorrhage might have had something to do with the C-section. My unfounded thoughts were feeding my journey of self-blame.

'OK, let me take a look at you,' Adonis said, manipulating bones in my body.

He worked on me for nearly an hour but I got no relief. Then looking at me in a non-apologetic way, he said, 'I'm not sure if osteopathy is going to be of benefit, but let me know how you are tomorrow.'

None of his interventions worked and over the following weeks, when he was unable to help with my pain, I thought it was my fault. My body couldn't be repaired.

But I didn't give up.

There must be something else? Perhaps acupuncture might mend me.

Kieran got the name of an acupuncturist, a Chinese man who lived in central Nicosia.

The Chinese are excellent acupuncturists, aren't they?

I had so much hope when we drove up outside a 1960s tower block in a rough part of the city.

There were health and safety issues accessing his clinic. Kieran had to lift Dylan and me over rubble and rusted steel bars to get into the lobby of his apartment block. Dirt and graffiti on the corridors and in the lift attempted to corrode my confidence. But I wouldn't let doubt creep in. I needed this to work.

Kieran knocked on the door of Apartment Number 15. No reply. He knocked again. Still no reply.

'Are we in the right place?' I asked him, just as the door opened.

'Hello,' said a small man who had a quiet arrogance about him. 'Come. Sit here. Why you here for acupuncture?'

I sat down slowly and looked over his shoulder at two yellow stained-glass doors which were off the small stuffy room.

What magic lurked behind those doors?

'I had a brain haemorrhage,' I replied, quickly turning my attention towards Dylan who was crying. He was waiting for Kieran to make up a bottle to feed him.

'How many time ago?'

'Six weeks.'

He approached me and looked at my arm and leg.

'OK I know what to do. I had many persons like this in China.'

'Can you help Kim?' Kieran asked from a couch near the door we'd just come through.

'Are you go for physiotherapy?'

154

'Yes, of course.'

'I think that not a good thing. You should do acupuncture always.'

'What do you mean?'

'Physiotherapy not will work.'

'But they're teaching me to walk.'

'I make you good. See me each two days every week for three months.'

'I'm not stopping physio, no matter what.'

By the end of the twelve weeks of sessions I hadn't improved to the extent the acupuncturist had believed I would and he told me there was no point returning. I blamed myself again.

What have I done?

At every corner there was somebody with their hand out telling me they could fix me. In desperation I paid out thousands of euros to people who couldn't cure me. When their therapies didn't work, I always thought it was my fault. I was in the 'bargaining' stage of grief – if I had taken more care of myself this wouldn't have happened.

I was worthless as a woman and as a mother.

My shame

THE hot sun shone through the glass roof and penetrated the steel rafters of the Mall of Engomi in one of Nicosia's shopping districts. Its direct heat lit up the restaurant table where I was sitting with two new acquaintances. Dylan was sucking on his soother in his buggy. Kieran had placed him beside me, before he'd sought ten minutes to browse around Debenhams.

'When are you going to go to the hydrotherapy pool?' Chrissy asked me.

'We're going on Saturday.'

'What will that entail?'

'I need to strengthen all of the muscles in my leg to help me to walk. The warm water should help with the movement.'

'Where's the pool?'

'It's only a few miles from where we're living in the UNPA, which is great.'

A stranger approached our table. She stood in front of the buggy, looked in at Dylan and started to smile.

'How old is the baby?'

'Two months,' Chrissy replied.

'He's a boy, I presume.'

'Yes.' I murmured, trying to catch this stranger's attention.

'What did you call him?'

156

The woman looked at my two friends at the table, assessing which one of them was the baby's mother.

'Dylan.' The three of us answered simultaneously.

'He's wonderful, many congratulations to you,' she said again, nodding their way.

This outsider didn't look at me once.

Sitting in a wheelchair can bring out discriminatory assumptions in people. My disability caused anxiety and many didn't know how to cope with the situation, thus unintentionally offending me. Part of me understood this as I may have had the same reaction before my disability, but on this occasion I was hurt.

The repulsive, friendly stranger never thought I was the baby's mother. She fussed over him the way women do when they see new-borns in public. He was mine but I felt people didn't think a woman who was wheelchair dependent would be able to give birth to a baby. I looked in at Dylan who was sleeping soundly and I reached my hand towards his leg. I stroked his soft skin. His eyes flickered open, I stared into them and we shared a moment of tenderness.

'No one will ever do that to us again,' I vowed. 'No one will dismiss our bond in such an abhorrent way. I'll make sure, little one.'

The following Saturday was my first exercise session in a hydrotherapy pool.

'Let's go!' I shouted to Kieran through the open window in the car.

I had been looking at him in the side-mirror of the passenger seat and was watching as he attempted to tightly pack Dylan's pram and my wheelchair into the boot of the car, before we set off on our fiftenn-minute journey.

As a childless couple we had splashed out on a smart black BMW Coupé. We'd had a list of extras fitted; a bluetooth hands-free set, air conditioning, alloy wheels, adaptive headlamps and a whole lot more. The list was endless, unnecessary and of little functional importance, but when we were on the forecourt we had been lured with talk of personal-customising and resale value.

The car had been purchased when we had no idea it would have to fit a pram and a mobility aid in its impractical boot.

A boot in a coupé is meant for bouquets of red roses, shopping or weekend suitcases.

Now the interior spec, the must-have sun-roof and the beige Dakota leather seats felt like vulgar excesses and I no longer inhaled the strong leather smell nor sat with pride in the front seat. Its gleaming metallic coat meant nothing and the time spent getting the interior valeted each week seemed to have been a ludicrous indulgence.

My materialistic ways had been ambushed. Things like this didn't matter to me anymore. I'd more pressing priorities.

Was my illness punishment for my self-obsessions? Maybe I deserved this to happen. But I didn't deserve being taken away from my week-old baby.

The noise at the rear of the car made me look in the side mirror again and I watched as the left wheel came off the wheelchair and Kieran angrily kicking it.

'This fuckin' thing!' he shouted at the top of his voice.

It's all my fault. If only, if only...

When I was in hospital he had driven around Nicosia to find a medical-supply shop which specialised in disability aids. Wheelchairs were lined up in a similar fashion to the way prams had been in Mothercare a lifetime ago, smaller ones at the front and larger to the back. Kieran had deliberated over the most suitable wheelchair and had reluctantly paid the shop assistant our holiday money for it. It wasn't about the money – for him the wheelchair represented the utter injustice of our situation. He had said to me, 'I was in that shop crying. I shouldn't have had to buy a wheelchair for my wife when we were supposed to be starting our lives as new parents with our infant son.'

Kieran temporarily fixed the wheel and got into the car. I could see he was exhausted as he'd been up a few times during the night both feeding Dylan and bringing me to the bathroom. Bags under his once bright-eyes and crow's feet were appearing on his face, faster than they should. During this time, he kept silent when he must have been feeling overwhelmed with sadness, stress and worry. Unfortunately there wasn't space in our relationship for him to express how he was feeling. It was all about me and my illness. When any of his family came to Cyprus to help, I warned them that he

159

might explode in utter anguish, and direct some of his fury at them.

He never did.

However, today the wheelchair was getting the brunt of it.

As we drove in silence from the safety of the house, I looked out of the window and studied the gargantuan Turkish flag which was dug into the Turkish military-occupied Kyrenia Mountainside, to the north of the UNPA. The flag was the size of twelve football-pitches and looked down on the south of Nicosia. Its imposing effect must have incensed many Greek Cypriots living in the south who had to look at it. Like it or not, the flag was impressive.

The Cypriot Problem resonated with me more than ever. I now understood what invasion meant. I had also been invaded by another force. I too was divided in half. Both the island and I were in turbulence and may never accept our malign occupation. No successful deal might be brokered in the near future. We had no choice but live with the fallout of gross invasion.

I was still feeling upset that I'd caused Kieran's anger so I purposely didn't look at him during the short journey. Soon the building appeared in the distance. Kieran parked in front of the entrance and an elderly man stepped in front of the car, opened the door and helped me into my wheelchair.

'Kalimera, you're welcome. Come this way and I'll show you everything,' he said kindly, diffusing the tension there had been between us in the car.

We followed him into the building and he showed us which way to go. Kieran brought Dylan and me into a dressing-room and he dressed me in my black maternity togs. They were hideous. Once they had been large enough to cover my ever-expanding expectant tummy – now I could have fitted two of me in them. But they were all I had. My objective was to learn how to walk. I wasn't fashion-conscious any longer. It wasn't a time to use my body to catch anyone's attention in the pool area: quite the opposite.

I implore you. Stop gawking. Avert your eyes.

Eris, my 20-year-old therapy instructor, helped me onto a seat which was connected to an electric hoist and lowered me into the small warm pool.

'You can get off now,' she explained. 'I'm coming in with you.'

I shimmied off the plastic chair into the water. My knuckles were white as I held onto a rail, fearful I'd completely submerge and be unable to resurface. Eris nimbly slithered in beside me and I couldn't help but notice her tanned-athletic physique next to mine. Once again I was reminded of my shattered body.

Please don't let there be a mirror close by. I couldn't bear looking at myself beside her.

She smiled at me and in that second I felt hope.

Come on Kim. You're strong, you're beautiful and you're amazing. Keep working hard and you'll be fixed. Give yourself time and everything will be back to normal. You've only lost function in an arm and a leg. You'll be fine: your baby needs you.'

161

I wanted so much to believe my internal words of support.

'I will hold your knee straight so you can put weight on your leg,' Eris said softly, bending down into the water.

I shifted my weight from one leg to the other and with her help I gradually limped around the small periphery of the tiny square pool.

'Eris, can you put on the water?' I asked some time later.

I was tiring and I was in pain.

The strong water-jets were turned on and I stood with my bottom up against the pressure of the water which was shooting from the side wall of the pool. My muscles were temporarily numbed giving me some relief.

I exercised like this for a while, stretching and using the pressurised-jets. By the time I was hoisted out of the water and dressed, I felt good about my workout.

'Time for food.'

We drove into the city-centre and found a trendy bistro called 'Seventh Heaven.' My arm was in a sling because over the weeks the loss of strength in the muscles around my shoulder was causing my arm to drop (sublux). A little gap appeared between my shoulder and arm and a new pain was emerging. I tried using a sling to relieve the shoulder pain but the pain shifted to my neck instead.

I prayed I didn't look like I'd had a brain haemorrhage or, worse still, a stroke. (I was beginning to resign myself that I'd have to start accepting the word *stroke* in relation to my illness and reluctantly began to use it.) Instead I wanted to resemble someone who'd been involved in a car crash. In recent years

Cyprus had more road fatalities than Ireland, so I tried to convince myself I bore a resemblance to one of the many casualties I had observed during the year. Being involved in a car crash was less shameful and more acceptable than being a stroke victim. Young people had car crashes, old people had strokes. Women gave birth without incident; older mums put themselves at risk. Doctors may have rejected my theory but I knew it was my fault and I was ashamed.

Foliage and pink geraniums fell from trellises at the entrance of this hip and trendy bistro. Outdoor couches with white cushions, sun umbrellas and art-deco lamps all boosted the beauty of the terrace of the eatery.

Saturday afternoons were special for us as a family. When my hydrotherapy sessions finished, we returned to this sanctuary each week for lunch. My digestive system was back working, so eating a large Greek salad was no longer such an ordeal to me. I still watched every morsel of food going into my mouth lest I suffer the same lack of dignity I'd experienced in the hospital, when my bowels were blocked for three weeks and intervention was needed. My husband had witnessed something no lover is supposed to see, but I would have done the same for him. After all, we'd signed the same contract: 'In sickness and in health.'

Dylan was asleep in the armchair between Kieran's couch and mine. We were beaming over our baby and it felt good. Most of our conversations during the week were about the losses and fallout we were enduring. On Saturdays I attempted to leave my distress behind.

Saturday afternoons were about Dylan.

'Look how big he's got.' I said, stroking the tiny cuticles of his fingernails. 'That was so funny yesterday when you put him in the clothes' basket and lifted him by the bungee weighing-scales. He's such a buster. Did you see him rolling out when you dropped the basket back onto the floor? I thought he'd hurt his head.'

'We've so many friends who have boys the same age. It's going to be crazy in a few years' time when they're all school-goers.'

'What school do you think we'll send him to?'

Our conversation continued in this normal manner and it felt good to put my desolation to one side. Dylan was the glue which kept us together during this time and he deserved adulation in the same way other babies do.

We needed to demonstrate to him how a family-unit worked in both good and difficult times. Even though Dylan had been born into a tenuous situation, he was learning that love and family were paramount. He was witnessing our family dealing with difficulties, so it was only fair that laughter and happiness were a balancing part of his life too. His innocent soul needed it. He was our future.

We loved him more than he would ever know. I had to give him the best.

I needed to learn to walk for him.

First steps

THE light was flickering in the basement room in the physiotherapy clinic. I was lying on my back and Andry was kneeling beside me. I looked up at the bright halogen light on the ceiling. The realisation of my situation began to dawn on me.

Is this the end of my life? My heart's broken in two. My baby is without his Mum.

Suddenly, I heard a loud noise and I turned my head. Rasmus, one of the patients, had fallen onto the floor near me and his body was trembling. Andry jumped up to remove his walking stick, on which he'd fallen. He was shaking violently and began to froth at the mouth.

I always liked Rasmus. He had been a photographer before his stroke but now like me, he was hemiplegic. He had told me his career was over – *un fait accompli*.

As suddenly as the seizure had started, it was over. Rasmus lay there stunned and it took him a while to come around.

'Are you OK, Kim?'

'Yes, of course,' I replied, surprised Andry asked me how I was doing when Rasmus was the one who needed attention.

'You know these seizures can happen.'

'Really?' I said nonchalantly, torn between my sympathy for Rasmus but also waiting for my physiotherapy session to continue.

165

When Rasmus was lucid again, Andry returned to the floor mat, and pulled my arms simulating sit-ups. My core muscles were still very weak and she did her utmost to strengthen them.

'Let's continue with your arm,' she said.

'I'm ready.'

Andry took my effected arm and placed it horizontally from my body.

'It's hurting, Andry.'

'You must to do this to keep your muscles working.'

'But my shoulder is very sore.'

'Will I stop?'

'No.'

'Find a way,' she encouraged.

This was Andry's motto 'find a way.' I knew I couldn't give up when she said these words.

If pain was going to help the muscles come alive again, then I'd persevere.

'When will my arm work again?' I asked, trying to take my mind off the piercing darts which were shooting from my scapula to my shoulder.

'You be patient.'

I knew not to delve deeper. I wasn't ready to hear the truth.

Some larger muscles were over compensating for the smaller non-working muscles, which was causing even more pain in my hip and bottom.

'Kim, take something to help you through this,' members of my family had said on numerous occasions.

I'm not taking painkillers or any other medication. I'll become addicted to them and I'll spend years trying to wean myself off.

I was foolish not to take medication which could help me. I now regret I never did. I think that those few months would have been easier had I not been so determined to do everything on my own. Sometimes a little help is needed in recovery and if painkillers, anti-depressants or sleeping tablets can alleviate some of the adversity, then asking for them might have been worth compromising my principles.

So I remained in pain.

I remained sad.

And I remained tired.

Kostas approached me and said, 'Now come to the treadmill I will practise you walking.'

I followed him and I stood still as he put a canvas support-harness around my lower abdomen. The harness-straps were connected to a hoist and when he pulled the straps, I was lifted airborne over the treadmill.

I had to be suspended in such a manner because I hadn't the strength to stand upright. Kostas lowered the height of the straps and I thumped down onto the treadmill. He supported my left leg and moved my foot to replicate a walking movement. I couldn't do it on my own, but I was being shown what to do.

'Come on Keem. Hurry, hurry, and concentrate hard. Bend the leg, hip hitch, heel and toe.'

Whoa! Information overload! What's he talking about? Why is he nagging me so much? I'm doing my best.

I was reminded of my French experiences on the ski slopes in the Alps: 'Bend z knees Keem.' I had done an exchange with a French girl, Marie, when I was a teenager in a vain attempt to learn French.

Skiing was not a natural talent of mine. I got the hang of parallel turns but because of my fear of heights, I never graduated past the intermediate class – much to the chagrin of my host family who black-sloped all day long.

I think I was always an embarrassment to them, with my 80s perm and dressed in my aunt's very untrendy ski gear. Brands like Louis Voutoin and Christian Dior rolled off their tongues as Dunnes and Penneys did in our house.

I smiled to myself and started to focus.

With Kostas' and Andry's persistence I was learning to walk. They had a formula and approached walking exercises from many angles. Daily passive and active muscle-strengthening exercises, an electronic muscle stimulator and a treadmill were just some of their tools.

'Well done Keem, you are learning to put weight on your leg. It's important to lock your knee in place so it doesn't bend and you don't fall,' Andry said a week later.

'Don't let me go.'

'You can do it on your own. Stand for five seconds.'

'Andry, don't let me go. I haven't locked my knee. I can't do it.'

'Find a way.'

'I'm trying.'

'I know you can put weight on your leg. Stand up straight. You can do this. Five seconds.'

I leant to my left but refused to let go of Andry.

'That was not good. Trust yourself, you won't fall. I'm here, I won't let you go.'

Dylan needs me to stand.

'Yes go: 1, 2, 3, 4. Bravo Keem, you found a way! Tomorrow, we will do more.'

'Thank you Andry for believing in me.'

We hugged. I lost my balance and fell on her pushing her against the wall.

'You work very hard.'

Soon the focus of my therapy began to change. Kostas was able to remove the harness-straps which had bitten into my groin, caused great discomfort and rubbed against my Caesarean incision.

I was ready to take a few steps.

'I hold this side, Andry you here,' Kostas said to his wife, pointing to the right of me. 'Keem you must do this, flex the knee, hip hitch, heel and toe.'

'It's too hard.'

'You can. I'm getting cross! Do it! We are practising this for weeks. If you can stand on your own, you can walk.'

This could change everything. I'll be normal again if I can walk. I will no longer need my wheelchair and people will treat me the way they used to. If it's the last thing I do today, I'll take a few steps. Dylan, I'm getting better: Mummy's coming back to you.

I put my heel on the floor and took a half step. I caught Andry out of the corner of my eye who was smiling at Kostas.

'Do it again.'

I did.

'And again.'

'You are walking!' Kostas cried. 'Andry you let go and I will hold Keem's hand.'

'I can't believe it Kostas, look at me!'

'Yes I see you. Bravo! Wait there, I want to give you something.'

I plonked down on a chair, turned my head and noticed Rasmus sitting close to me.

'Good, good, happy,' he declared, smiling.

I can walk. I did it. I can walk!

'This is the present,' Kostas said handing me a tripod stick.

'Wow!'

'Go and try again.'

I stood up and took the stick from Kostas. I allowed my fingers massage the hard plastic handle. My stick was my prize. I had qualified – passed my test.

I placed the stick to the right of me and leaning heavily on it, I dragged my weak leg to the side and took a step. There was no need for Kostas to hold me. I was independent. I took three more steps and then sat down with exhaustion. I couldn't wait for Kieran to return to collect me. He was due any minute. I knew he'd be proud.

Hope was increasing.

Suddenly I saw him coming through the door down the corridor, towards me.

'Kieran, Kieran, I took some steps! Watch!'

I was ecstatic as I shuffled slowly across the corridor taking calculated strides.

'You are amazing! Look what you've achieved in less than two months.'

His eyes were watery and he was hugging me tightly.

'Do it again.'

'I'm thrilled Kieran. I'm walking. Dr Buros said I'd be walking and I am. I know my walk is very different to before but I don't care. I'm really proud of myself. I can't wait to show Ann when I get back to the house. Mum's coming over next week and I'll be able to show her I can walk. I'll say nothing to Mum until then. She'll be so happy!'

Things were looking up. It was just going to take time. I practised my new walk non-stop and when the pain got too much, I kept going. When I kept going, the pain got too much. It was a vicious circle but I needed to walk.

Help from our families

'SHE'S coming out of arrivals now, so we'll be about an hour. I'll send you a text when we're entering through the gate at UNPA,' Ann whispered down the phone.

'Thanks. Remember, say nothing.'

'I won't.'

An hour later the doorbell rang loudly. I was in position at the end of the corridor. My heart was on fire and I was trembling. I had been practising my performance for a week and I wanted it to be perfect.

'Hello! We're here!' Ann shouted.

My cue.

Using every resource I had, I started on what seemed like the biggest journey of my life. I put one foot in front of the other. My internal voice was coaxing me, 'flex, hip, heel and toe. Walk.'

I kept my head down to look at my feet and rigorously walked the length of the corridor, before collapsing into Mum's arms. It was a huge feat and I was filled with pride. I had done it! My concerted effort had been fruitful. I was no longer completely reliant on a wheelchair.

'You're walking my love, I can't believe it! My little girl, you've achieved the impossible.'

Barely making out what she was saying through her frenzied sobs, I sniggered, 'Oh my God Mum, calm down.'

I looked over at Ann.

'This is like her hysterical-convulsions when we brought her to see *When a Man loves a Woman*, over fifteen years ago.'

We had been mortified back then in the cinema and I had elbowed Mum in the ribs to tell her to be quiet. Parents have that effect of really letting you down in public and that had been one of those moments. But now Mum had every right to be emotional – after all, her youngest daughter had walked ten-feet for the first time since she'd last seen her.

I was so happy with my achievement and was delighted she was the one who was with me during the height of this event. Mum was offering invaluable support, so naturally she was one of the first people I wanted to witness this triumph.

When other members of our two families came to Cyprus, I showed them my progress. Their smiles spurred me on. They were there for us during those important months and were integral in my early recovery. They gave all of their time to us and never made us aware of their needs during those unconditionally devoting visits.

There was so much we needed them to do for us. I was reliant on someone to get me showered and dressed in the morning. Dylan needed the same attention. I needed nurturing when I was upset, so did Dylan. I needed help in and out of my wheelchair – Dylan needed help in and out of his pram.

We were dependent on others and Kieran needed help too.

At Hallowe'en, my brother Philip arrived for five days. It was so lovely seeing him and I felt bad that this, his first visit to Cyprus was under such strained circumstances. He wasn't over on a holiday, he never got to see any of the places Kieran and I used to go – there was even flash flooding while he was there. Had he been given the opportunity; the aridness of the land, the live-stock and the island's history would have enthralled him but I needed him more than the island needed him. He came to be with me and regretfully I wasn't able to share him.

He was still stable, loving Philip and he showed he cared by sharing his tears with mine. His condolence lay in his silence, his eye contact and the big hugs he gave me. I would never know how much he cared.

The precious little brother whom I'd always adored.

A few weeks before he'd come over, I'd overheard my mother on the phone trying to reassure Philip that he didn't need to travel the long distance to me if it didn't suit.

'Honestly Philip, there's no need. We're doing all we can here, love. You've enough on your plate at home with the kids and the farm. What do you think? If you want to come, do, but don't feel you have to. It's up to you.'

I hope Philip comes. He wants to come. He needs to come. He has a right to witness all that's happening to his sister. If the shoe were on the other foot I'd want to be here. When things weren't looking good for me, he had to stay behind to mind the farm. It must have been hard for him saying goodbye to Dad and Carla when they were summoned to Cyprus just before my operation.

I was coming from an altruistic place when I spoke to Philip on the phone and asked him to visit me. I knew he wanted to come to be part of the family support. I wanted him to know that he mattered in all of this too. He could help and he was very much wanted.

Kieran's mother and two of his brothers also came to help and we were both grateful for the sacrifices they had made.

Like Kieran, they were great with children, so when Kieran's oldest brother, Martin, arrived for a week we were very happy to leave Dylan in his capable hands to do the night feeds.

Kieran's Mum closed her B&B business for the week she spent with us. Always the doting Granny, she lovingly cared for Dylan during the day, before she'd reluctantly hand him back at night. She was a motherly support and her love for Kieran manifested itself in the love she showed for a special grandchild she thought she'd never have.

David, the youngest of Kieran's family, gave us two weeks. His nickname was Jamie Oliver and for the time he spent with us, we ate like lords. He minded Dylan and cared for Kieran, his older brother. The tables had turned. Kieran had once minded David when he was a baby and now David was minding him.

I was only their daughter/sister-in-law and yet they treated me as though I were blood related. Their practical and

175

emotional help was invaluable and I know their encouragement was also important to Kieran's feeling of self-worth.

Even though Kieran hadn't asked for support, his family recognised he needed help and was there for him.

Guy Fawkes

THE evening after David's departure, Tina arrived into our lives. She was a Garda, was living close-by, and wanted to help us out in her own thoughtful way. A small, cheerful woman from the Midlands, Tina became our Guardian Angel of sorts.

Tina never took no as an answer, and when she arrived up to our house one late, dark autumnal evening with a box of Scrabble in hand, she insisted the three of us sit around the kitchen-table and play a game. Board games were the last thing on my mind but there was no way out. She was dogged.

'Get rid of that plate off the table,' she demanded, taking letters out of the box and placing them upside down on the lid of the box, 'and move the pram into the hall. Kieran bring over that chair. What's that depressing music?'

'Damien Rice.'

She started to laugh.

'Are you serious? Turn it off and put on something more uplifting! You have yourselves hidden away from everyone and Damien Rice will only make you feel worse.'

Tina said we had to turn off the CD player, so we turned it off. She said we'd to play Scrabble so we played four games.

Kieran was losing terribly and was becoming disenchanted, so he started to concoct bizarre words which were making Tina and me snigger.

'There you go, you laughing hyenas! How many points do I get for that word?' Kieran said, placing letters in a line on the board.

'"Quizzy" isn't a word!'

'It's an abbreviation of inquisitive.'

'Yeah right. It's me who's missing one sixth of my brain, not you.'

Kieran and Tina looked at each other and smiled. It was the first time they heard me joking about my brain injury and they were pleased for me. We all started to laugh and during the rest of the game my disability dissipated and I enjoyed myself.

From then on Tina came to the house and occasionally dragged me down to the pub to meet our Irish friends. Nothing was going to impede her persistence. She assisted me in and out of her car without a second thought. She was a breath of fresh air in our lives and helped us through many difficult hours. Her jovial manner was heartening and I enjoyed her in-your-face personality.

Our social calendar was beginning to take off, which was imperative to me at that time and was important for my emotional recovery. The small liberation from our day-to-day lives was probably even more beneficial to Kieran who needed others around him. Watching him with a pint of Guinness and chatting about UN issues with other Gardaí was great to see and eased my conscience for having caused him so much pressure and distress.

The new Irish Contingent was wonderful and came to our assistance at every turn. If any of our family members needed to be collected or dropped off at Larnaca airport, they volunteered to drive the two hour round-trip to assist us. Much to our delight, dinner invitations were frequent. They also called in regularly, ran errands and minded Dylan and me, which all lightened Kieran's load.

The two Irish Contingents deserved a Nobel Prize in kindness.

One evening in early November Tina brought Kieran and me home from the local pub.

'I'll be back tomorrow before the party,' were her departing words.

'What's she talking about?' I asked Kieran.

'I've no idea.'

The next day after my afternoon nap I could hear Tina's voice in the kitchen telling Kieran the British Contingent had invited us all to a Guy Fawkes bonfire in a field in the UNPA.

'I'm not going!' I shouted to her.

'Oh yes you are.'

'I'm in too much pain.'

'Take some Panadol. We're leaving in a few minutes.'

This woman was incorrigible! Could she not leave me alone?

The kitchen door was flung open and I was blinded by a life-size Buzz Light Year.

'Oh my God, Tina, what are you wearing? You're crazy!'

'I've brought a Minnie Mouse costume for you and a cute little Noddy outfit for Dylan too.'

My eyes welled up. I was trying really hard to be upbeat but it was too hard. I couldn't do it anymore. The thought of attending this event for a few hours, having no choice but to sit in a wheelchair, wasn't nice. Further exposition by dressing up as a Disney character was definitely out of the question.

'You don't have to go, Kim.'

'That's really nice of you to say Kieran, but I'll go.'

Kieran, Tina and Dylan were going to the event. I couldn't make them stay at home with me and ruin the experience for them.

Buzz Light Year and Noddy sat in the back of the car without a self-conscious care in the world, while the driver and his passenger pretended to embrace the night ahead.

We parked the car close to the gate and I got into the wheelchair.

'Wow look at that!' Buzz shouted, making Kieran and me jump.

I looked up.

The smell of smoke bellowing from the 20-foot-high bonfire had struck me even before I noticed the stalls selling candyfloss and drinks. Hot-dog stands were busy and there were queues of people waiting to go into a tent.

'I'm going to find some of the others. Are you OK Kim?' Tina asked, bending down and giving my cold hand a rub.

'Yes, I'm good. This is amazing!'

'See you soon.'

She went off and blended perfectly into the crowd of toads and witches. The three of us were left alone trying to take in the spectacle. A member of the Britcon came over to us. He shook Kieran's hand and Kieran introduced him to me.

'This is Paul. He has been brilliant organising our house.'

'Thank you so much,' was all I could say. I was grateful to this man and I held him in high esteem.

'I hope everything is alright with your accommodation,' Paul said to us both. 'If there's anything we can do to make things easier for you just let me know and I'll see what can be done.'

'Thanks Paul. Do you know where we can buy firewood? Kim's always cold and we need to get some to keep the fire going at night.'

'Sorted!'

And that was that. The Britcon sorted out everything for us.

The offers of help from their wives poured in too.

'I'm a beautician. Would you like me to wax your legs or paint your toe nails?'

'I do massage, I'll be over tomorrow and give you a rub down to see if I can help with your pain.'

'I've loads of magazines, I'll bring them over.'

We were treated like one of the British families who were living in the UNPA. We were invited to some of their functions and were minded as their own. Tonight's invitation to their Guy Fawkes celebrations was an example of their hospitality and care.

The bonfire was raging furiously and I could make out some spectacular fireworks shooting into the sky in the background. I was looking through the crowds of excited children and adults when I noticed some vaguely-familiar-looking women approaching.

'Hi do you remember me?' one of them asked.

I nodded, not really knowing if I'd met her before or not.

She took Dylan from Kieran's arms and I could see her fingers stroking Dylan's little nose as it stuck out from under the blue Noddy hat. She passed Dylan around between her and the other two women and I was touched by their complimentary words.

Kieran left with Paul and I was alone with the women who were still ogling over Dylan, rubbing his face and caressing his tiny un-gloved hand. They chatted among themselves.

'He's really cute. Did you see that smile?'

'I know and look at his little costume, it's so gorgeous.'

'He reminds me of my baby when she was three months old.'

'I hope he's warm enough.'

'Has he a dirty nappy?'

'No I think he's fine.'

'I really think he should have more layers on. I used to put two jackets on my baby when she was small.'

OK, that's enough. Hand him back to his Mummy.

No one knew my turmoil. I wanted him so much but was overwhelmed by the cackle of women towering over me. I was afraid to ask for him to be returned because I was scared that if Dylan accidently slumped over in my arm, there would be a fuss, and once again he'd be swept away. All I could do was watch and fight back my tears.

I waited and waited.

182

'Will I pop him on your lap?'

I looked up at Buzz Light Year who had rescued Dylan from his admiration society.

'Thanks Tina.'

I relaxed and started to stroke Dylan's cold ruddy cheek. I rubbed my red-tipped nose on his and whispered, 'Remember, I'm your Mummy.'

Leaving Cyprus behind

IN November and December, when I was at physiotherapy, Kieran spent much of his time on the phone trying to get me into the National Rehabilitation Hospital (NRH) in Dublin. It was imperative for me to continue my rehabilitation on my return to Ireland. The medics in Cyprus had saved my life, the physiotherapists had got me walking and I needed to keep going at the same pace. I worried that if I didn't get admitted to the NRH that I'd be coming back to Cyprus for more physiotherapy. Kostas and Andry specialised in working with those who'd had strokes and I hoped their expertise would be replicated in Dublin.

I had to get in.

In Ireland it can be who you know that counts and Kieran contacted as many people as he could to help get me a place in the NRH. Our local T.D. was lobbied and three other politicians were approached by some of our family members.

Kieran spent two full months sending e-mails, letters and reports. Most days he was on the phone to HSE personnel and if he wasn't badgering someone, he was in Cypriot hospitals looking for x-rays, MRI and CT scans which were needed by the relevant agencies in Ireland. He had to go back and forth to Nicosia General Hospital to ask my neurosurgeons to write reports which would assist in securing me a bed in the NRH. It was a hard time for him as he met many hurdles on the way. Medical scans needed to be accompanied by reports and reports needed to be accompanied by scans.

Silly, nit-picking bureaucracy.

Friends of ours in Ireland contacted 'those in the know' who might help with information which was needed for reports. Kieran was becoming proficient at the bureaucratic process and to hurry things up, he started to draft medical reports himself and brought them to relevant doctors to be authenticated and signed.

And then he'd to find out which HSE area in Ireland had the best reputation for fast-tracking patients to the NRH. Should our address be Killaloe in County Clare or, Ballina in County Tipperary? After all, we did live in a twin town in two separate counties. We didn't mind what county we said we lived in. Either would do. As a matter of fact, any county would do.

One morning in early December, I was on a plinth working with Kostas, when I heard footsteps pounding down the corridor.

'You've got in!' Kieran shouted, running through the door where Kostas and I were. 'We've to go home in five days' time.'

Kostas and I looked at him in disbelief. It meant the end of our therapist-client relationship and my sixteen months in Cyprus. It was time to take Dylan home to his extended family and to finally put down our roots and start afresh.

'I'm so happy to you. You must to go, it's time,' Kostas spluttered.

I'll miss you Kostas. I'm terrified of leaving your country and heading into the unknown.

'Go now and book you aeroplane to Dublin.'

There was pandemonium over the next few days, packing, booking final appointments with doctors and saying goodbye. But there was yet one huge hurdle to overcome: the pain. I wouldn't be able to sit in an aeroplane for five hours.

I'd no choice. I had to give in and see a pain specialist. He prescribed me anti-inflammatories. The drugs worked and from that week on my pain reduced considerably.

Why didn't I go to him before this? Why was I so stubborn?

The home-coming was approaching and I was starting a new chapter of my life: a chapter I was dreading.

I want to stay. I want to hide away. I want Andry and Kostas to mend me. Who's going to take care of me and Dylan in Ireland? I still can't care for Dylan and he'll be taken from me. I'll be alone.

It was time to face my demons.

It was quiet in the taxi when we were driving out the gate of the UNPA for the very last time. I took a final look at the Turkish Cypriot flag on the northern mountains and I breathed a sigh of relief that I'd never have to travel across the border into northern Cyprus again. In recent months when we'd family over, Kieran had brought them to Kyrenia and Famagusta to see a little of the Turkish-occupied part of the island. Those trips held memories of anguish, and I never looked forward to them. The bleakness of the less developed part of the island attracted some tourists, but it just wasn't

186

alluring to me. But then again I was one of those people who prefer Dundrum Town Centre to the Sally Gap, or Galway city to the Burren.

But invariably I'd concede to the suggestion we'd go north for an afternoon trip. I knew it was the right thing to do; if people came to help, I couldn't expect them to stay in the house 24/7. So I'd sit in the car trying to converse, but I was really looking at Turkish lookout posts and at Turkish soldiers, hoping they'd shoot me and put an end to something that had an infinite hold over me.

I was never shot.

And now it was time to leave Cyprus for good.

'This is so difficult,' I said to Kieran when we were on the way to Larnaca airport.

The taxi was taking us through Pyla where I'd spent the best days of my life. Each road the car meandered down, each shop and house I saw held memories of happy times. Dams hadn't the strength to hold back flashbacks of joy, and the subsequent demise of that happiness caused turbulent volumes of tears to plummet down my face.

'Yes you're right. It's hard to see it all again and remember the times we spent in our house, in our friends' houses and in Andy's Bar.'

My mouth was padlocked and I couldn't answer. The good memories were like daggers piercing my body, much worse than any ache I'd had up to this.

'But I'm not better. I'm not better.'

'You're walking Kim. The muscles in your arm will probably come back over the next few months. The physios in the NRH might be able to do things which Andry and Kostas overlooked. Keep up that same hope you've bravely retained up to this. You're a wonder and I'll always be in awe of you.'

His words couldn't console me. I hadn't recovered. I had worked hard for four and a half months, thinking I'd be better on my return. I'd thought that if I put effort into my rehabilitation I'd go home with a perfectly healed body. It hadn't happened.

Part
Three

The journey home

THE aeroplane was the apron and from my new vantage point I saw the steps lined up against the fuselage. I was 20 feet in the air on a hydraulic lift which was bringing me towards the rear of the plane. I needed to be in my wheelchair for parts of the long journey home as the few feet I was able to walk wasn't sufficient to get me up flights of steps or through airports. No one was allowed to board until I was settled into a seat at the front of the plane and my wheelchair was stored away.

'In an emergency you'll be last to get off the plane,' an air steward said to me sympathetically as she helped me into my seat. Her aviation rule (whether officially true or not) simply confirmed my growing belief that people with disabilities are a burden on society and able-bodied are more worthy of life.

Following a successful four-and-a-half hour flight, we got off the plane in London and went to collect our luggage. I sat near the conveyor-belt watching everything in slow motion. People were furiously trying to find their luggage and I willed them to calm down and to stop stressing over small incidentals.

Slow down, relax. What is the worst that can happen? Getting delayed and missing a bus into London city centre? So what!

Dylan was on my lap and I was soothing him by jerking the wheelchair rhythmically with my heel on the tiled floor. Kieran removed our two large suitcases and placed them on a trolley and started to walk towards Dylan and me.

'Kieran, Dylan's slipping out of my arm. Kieran catch him!'

'OK give me a minute,' he said, exasperatedly manoeuvring the trolley, and shoving his heavy rucksack onto his back, 'For God's sake, give me a bloody minute!'

I lowered my head and using my chin to keep Dylan from falling, I resumed my thinking. It was my fault this had happened. It was my fault my baby wasn't being reared by his mother.

All my fault.

Dylan was in a sling snuggled into his father's chest and the rucksack was now propped on Kieran's back. He pushed the luggage trolley with his left hand and my wheelchair with the other. No one helped. Heathrow is that type of airport, where people fear other passengers: climates had changed and assisting others could be perilous.

We searched arrivals for Kieran's two English cousins who had come to the airport to assist us catch our connecting flight to Dublin.

'Kieran over here!' the younger of the two, Marian, shouted running towards us.

'Thank God you're here,' was all I heard from Kieran's shaky voice as he started to break down in tears, relieved he was no longer on his own.

'It's good to see you both and the baby,' Marian said sweetly, hugging Kieran and rubbing his back reassuringly.

The two women had been generous to Kieran and me years back when we had holidayed in London. Since then we had met them many times at weddings in Ireland, and we were pleased to see them once more.

Then looking down at me, Margaret whispered, 'Kim, I don't know what to say. You've been through so much. But look at your beautiful baby. You're blessed to have him.'

'I know, thanks.'

'You've forty minutes before you're boarding your flight to Dublin, come this way to the check-in desk. We know what gate the flight is leaving from. Let's go.'

Marian took the heavily-laden trolley from Kieran and Margaret pushed me.

There was little time for conversation in the rush of getting us through the airport. Without their help, we knew we would have missed our flight to Dublin.

They said their goodbyes at the gate, kissed us and headed home on the Tube. How I wished that were me.

I'm getting closer, very soon everyone will know what happened.

Coming home was becoming a reality and I was in turmoil. Kieran's cousins were the first members of our extended family who had just witnessed my disability and whilst they were very kind, I hated them seeing me the way I was.

It's going to be humiliating. There's no hiding now. I've been found out. Everyone will know I did something wrong to cause a stroke.

Even though our flight was slightly delayed, the air stewards didn't rush us. They had been informed of our impending arrival and were prepared with kindness. No passengers were boarded until we were seated and coffee was served to us.

Dylan cried for the first time since our departure from Cyprus. He had slept the whole way from Larnaca to Heathrow but now, perhaps as my anxiety was increasing, he too was becoming agitated.

We ensured he was always surrounded by people who loved him, by people who cared. He was blanketed in love, love from us, love from our families and love from friends. He deserved the best and love is a worthy gift to give anyone. Nonetheless, however much you want to protect your child, there comes a time when it's impossible. Our situation was one of those times, I couldn't stop him from being upset and he probably needed to release some tension and cry.

'Let me take the baby,' one of the stewardesses said to Kieran, 'yes and the bottle. I've hot water to heat it up.'

'That would be brilliant. Thanks so much.'

The sudden influx of passengers put a halt to her assistance. She had to place Dylan on my lap and return the bottle to Kieran.

As soon as the plane took off, the final part of our journey began.

An hour later we heard:

'Ladies and gentlemen, you are very welcome to Dublin. The outside temperature is currently 3°C. For those of you who are returning to Ireland, welcome home, and for those of you who are holidaying here, we wish you a pleasant stay.'

No balloons, no friends and no 'Welcome Home' posters were there for us in arrivals. We weren't beaming or showing our little baby to family members for the first time. Instead, one of Kieran's Garda colleagues met us off the plane and helped us through the airport with as little fuss and delay as was possible. Being escorted through arrivals by a member of An Garda Síochána was a novel return to our country of origin.

My head was bent low.

Then I heard an unmistakable voice.

'Hi Kim.'

I looked up at my sister. 'Hi Ann.'

Doing time in the NRH

THE moon was out and there was still a lot of traffic on the M50 as people were returning to the safety of their homes after work. Ann was driving, bringing me back home to where my life had once started. She and my brother Philip were quiet in the car. My sobbing was silencing the usual airport-collection conversation of "How did your holiday go?"

Intuitively Ann said, 'What's it like for you being home?'

Like me, she never bothered with small talk – we got straight to the crux of the issue. Some people found our brevity unnerving but once they got to know us they usually reacted well when they realised we were genuinely interested in their welfare. Ann was doing just that. She wouldn't accept 'fine' as an answer and she, Philip and I knew how authentic the question was.

'I thought I'd be better. I have to look at old acquaintances in the eye and explain what happened. My clawed fingers mightn't ever straighten, my arm won't fuse into my shoulder, my scapula will always have to take the full weight of my arm and be sore and my leg might always have to be supported with an aid.

My anger and self-pity were increasing.

'I wish I could help but I do hear what you're saying.'

I knew she did, and I knew Philip heard it too. Whilst her words weren't helping my sorrow, it mattered that she asked and was listening. So I continued, 'More importantly, I'll have to accept the loss of not being the Mum I presumed I'd have been.'

That was my perpetual loss, losing precious time with my new-born. It wasn't fair and it wasn't right. A baby needs its mother and a mother needs her baby – it's nature's law. I would always be grateful to Dylan because he kept me going: he kept me alive and at some stage soon I would show him off to others in a slightly different way than I had planned, but with the same pride and love. He was teaching me how to live: he was curing me, but there was still loss.

We pulled into the driveway of my parents' house.

The central-heating was blasting through the open porch-doors as Kieran assisted me in on that cold winter's night. Mum came to the door and hugged me.

'You're home my pet. You're home.'

I stiffened, she was right. I was home to face the actuality of my life.

When I had trained as a psychotherapist, a decade before, I learned that shame is to guilt as hurt is to anger. I was hurt by my loss and the hurt made me angry. Or was it the other way around? I still blamed myself that my body hadn't been strong enough to stop the leaking blood in my brain, I was guilty of having a weak body and that guilt was increasing the shame I refused to relinquish. But whichever way it was, ultimately I felt shame – other people's bodies don't let them down, why mine?

I will always remember the first dinner I had at home with my family. It was nice seeing Dylan with his grandparents and they couldn't keep their eyes off him. I studied him closely when he was being passed from one person to the next and was gurgling with glee.

This particular night was different to any other meals I'd had over the years. I disappeared into myself and didn't know how to pull myself out of that darkness. If I'm honest, I didn't want to come out of the darkness. There was no light either inside or outside of me. What was the point?

I sat at the top end of the dining-table quiet and subdued. Polite conversation didn't mask the feeling of upset and love which was coming from my family, who didn't know what to say to get through to me. I was in my own world and Dylan and Kieran were the only ones who could drag me out of it. My life and I had changed. I was reliving the shock I had felt when I'd first left hospital. The stages of grief were hurtling towards me at full force and I had few recourses left to protect myself.

Post-traumatic Stress Disorder it's called, when you have been exposed to a traumatic event and your symptoms cause high anxiety levels. Apparently many sufferers avoid revisiting memories of the event. Whilst my symptoms included increased anxiety, I must have been on the opposite end of the spectrum when it came to avoidance of the incident. I couldn't stop talking about my traumatic event to my family and close friends, and even though I felt shame, in a perverse way I still needed people to know what happened to me. If they could witness my pain, they would show compassion and I could surrender a little of the humiliation I was so determined not to let go.

However, I wasn't ready to meet old acquaintances and watch the look of blame in their eyes. Family wouldn't judge, good friends would remain loyal, but old pals might see my culpability.

People tried hard to console me with kind gestures and sympathy. Deriving strength from their efforts helped me through the days and I was grateful to them. As unique individuals we can't ever experience another's pain so unfortunately no one was able to fill that missing piece of me and, no matter how many friends or strangers I told my story to, the vacuum was never filled. I was alone in my disgrace.

I was really nervous heading to the National Rehabilitation Hospital on my first morning after our return home. Kieran drove down Rochestown Avenue in Dublin on that inaugural day towards the institutional building, built at the beginning of the century. The NRH had been operating as a hospital for fifty years and was going to be my home for the next six weeks as an in-patient.

We pulled into the car park and Kieran and I walked up the ramp towards the front door. We saw the reception desk in the hallway of the old hospital entrance-hall. I walked towards the counter and waited for the receptionist to finish talking on the phone. I looked around the foyer at how the old was merged with the new. The convent building, which had been altered by modern extensions and necessary hospital-fixtures, must have been very beautiful at one time. I'd spent much of my educational and work life in convents and was always in awe of the opulent décor to be seen inside the doors. Here I felt that hidden behind the hospital façade, the Sisters of Mercy's influence would still be quite evident.

A sign for the chapel pointed towards the right and I knew it would be beautifully decorated like the convent chapels in which I had attended First-Friday Masses. For years, teachers had put their index finger to their lips gesturing me to keep quiet when I was a child and, for seventeen years of my teaching life, I had imitated their gesticulations trying to keep my own pupils in tow. Religious school-principals did not stand for bad behaviour in church and, whether you were a child or a teacher, you kept your mouth shut!

'Kim Maguire, brain injury, let me see; yes, St Bridget's Ward. Take the lift to the second floor and ask for the nurse on duty,' she said softly, pointing straight ahead.

We continued towards the lift. A teak banister, on an otherwise disappointingly plain staircase, rose from a linoleum-covered hospital floor. The wood provided a softness which was missing from the solidness of the old building. The polished banister was like the one on the staircase in my primary school, stairs which children were only allowed use during fire-drill and presumably during an actual fire. ('Single file please!')

Kieran and I didn't go up the stairs and instead got the lift to St. Bridget's Ward. It was all I had imagined. There were about ten beds, each surrounded by yellow curtains which were pulled back. The beds were side-to-side with individual lockers. Large windows brightened the ward with sunlight, and I could see signs over the beds with the name of the patient's rehabilitation consultant.

I dreaded being surrounded by patients who had similar brain injuries to me. I hadn't the armour to shield myself from others' emotions which could potentially penetrate the air and career towards me. I had to protect myself at all costs.

'We'll put you in a room on your own. Is that OK?' a nurse of similar age to me said.

'That's fine.'

'Come through this way and I'll get you set up.'

I followed the nurse past the Nurses' Station through the men's ward. Most of the beds were empty and I looked around trying to take some of it in. I scratched my nose, obstructing the smell of disinfectant and central-heating. It was a typical hospital smell and my thoughts of superior modern Cypriot hospitals were beginning to cloud my judgement. It was time for me to erase those memories and remind myself I was now back in Ireland, in an underfunded-public hospital and it just wasn't right to make comparisons between the two.

I was shown to one of the two single rooms which was situated on the other side of the main wards. I breathed a sigh of relief. I was grateful for the seclusion. Being able to spend time with my family in the privacy of that room in the evenings

201

was something very important to me and it was thoughtful of the nursing staff to think of my situation in such a human way.

'I'd better go and take Dylan from your Mum and let her get some rest,' Kieran said when he'd unpacked my bag and put my clothes into the bedside locker.

He assured me he'd return later that evening. My parents' house was only ten kilometres from the NRH and it wouldn't take him long to get to Glencullen and return within a few hours.

Kieran had built up weeks of work-holidays which were supposed to be used as part of our grand plan to tour Cyprus. Instead, these days were utilised to care for Dylan and me. With Mum now minding Dylan, Kieran was able to catch up with his family and friends. It was his turn to seek a little freedom and support.

Mum was thrilled to be able to help out and mind her youngest grandson but Kieran never relinquished control of Dylan and everyone, including Mum, was given strict instructions on how to feed, bathe and hold Dylan. His supervision was one of the small things in our life we had some control over. Kieran was doing this for me and for him. No matter what had happened, we were Dylan's parents and were grateful to people for respecting our wishes, regardless of how 'anal' those wishes were.

Following Kieran's departure, I sat alone on my bed and studied my therapy timetable for the week ahead. It didn't make much sense; everything was alien to me in this hospital.

After some time I decided to explore my surroundings. I walked back to the lift and descended to the ground floor.

Four corridors joined up together in a square shape and each corridor had large windows looking out onto an inner garden. The garden was well planted and if I had known anything about shrubs, I would have been able to sit back, admire and enjoy the colours and peacefulness it was trying to evoke.

Looking closer I saw some tall palm trees standing forlorn at the end of the garden. They weren't anything like the palm trees in the gardens of the exquisitely manicured grounds in the hotel in Pissouri. This was Ireland in freezing temperatures. Was a hospital garden with palm trees feebly trying to lure me into believing I was somewhere else and nothing had happened? If only it could.

I didn't know what to do so I ventured down a corridor and entered a large general-purpose room. It had a pool table in the middle of the room, and was otherwise empty except for a large TV. A replay of *EastEnders* was blaring from the box on the wall. How imposing. I hadn't watched TV in five months and resented its imposition. Most media fora and entertainment programmes now repulsed me. How could people actually watch such trivia, didn't they realise my life had ended? The poem by W.H. Auden resonated with me:

> '*Stop all the clocks, cut off the telephone,*
> *Prevent the dog from barking with a juicy bone,*
> *Silence the pianos and with muffled drum*
> *Bring out the coffin, let the mourners come.*'

I had often listened to the words of the poem during funerals in the past, and it was now my time to ask for the clocks to be stopped. My body was in the coffin and I was the mourner.

Quiet, turn off the TV and respect my loss.

I hadn't anywhere else to go and as I tried to shut out the cockney accents, I turned side-ways on the chair and gazed out the window. I was startled and saddened by the unexpected view. The reclaimed mountainous land of my home-place was staring me in the face. I had no idea I would be able to see the mountain I had been reared on. I stood up and leaning across a chair, I placed my hand on the window pane for a closer look.

The land was bare and I could just about see clusters of ewes feeding from large communal hay-wracks. No cattle were out grazing: they would be indoors for the winter. The farm-house wasn't visible anymore due to forty years' growth of conifers which had gradually blocked its view out over the city. Green galvanised sheds blended into the background and were not discernible from where I was standing.

This vista was akin to the view I had from the third floor in secondary school when I'd distractedly stare out my classroom windows. During the year the fields changed from a yellow-barley hue to a brown-black colour of pungent cow dung. The dark colour of the manure-doused fields would put a disgusted look on my face and I'd say nothing to my schoolmates about the possible stench my house might be engulfed in. As a teenager I didn't want to be on that hill but now it held everything which had been perfect. So near, yet so far.

The winter of 1980

TO be born in April in our house was not a cherished event. My brother Philip was born on the same date as me, three years later, and even the birth of a most-longed-for heir did not alter the poor timing of our birthdays. March and April were lambing months and all of the usual household activities were put on hold to 'do the lambing.'

When I was ten-years-old, the weather was particularly bad. The first lambs started to arrive on the bitter cold morning of St Patrick's Day. The forecast wasn't favourable for the week and my siblings and I knew there would be work to be done to help Mum and Dad. I was arguing with my two older sisters in the kitchen.

'You do it Kim,' Carla, the elder of the two told me.

'I'm not going to. Dad will freak!' I said. 'Ann you put it on.'

'No way! It's not even 12 o'clock yet. They go mad if we put the central-heating on before five.'

'I'll do it then, you're both such chickens!' Carla snarled at her two younger sisters, stomping up the hall to the dining-room to where the boiler-switch was tucked neatly away in a press with the underused antique china.

Ann and I looked at each other relieved. Carla would get the brunt of my parents' fury when they'd find out we were wasting home-heating oil.

The back door was flung open and Mum trudged wearily into the (now) warm kitchen carrying a new-born lamb. The fire in the stove was always ablaze for such helpless off-spring to heat up after their mothers had given birth to them on miserable, wet, spring days. This was one of those medical situations we were prepared for, and our emergency plan was put into action. I went upstairs and grabbed the hairdryer from the bathroom, Carla laid pages from the Farmers' Journal and the Sunday Independent in front of the old Rayburn-stove, and Ann searched for a decommissioned tea towel to dry the poor frozen creature.

Caked in mud, the lamb was carefully placed on the newspapers on the scorch-marked linoleum in front of the fire. His fleece was matted with a mixture of after-birth and snow and he was shivering. Ann bent over him and started to rub the muck off. I stood aside, hairdryer in hand ready to dry him when Ann was finished her procedure.

'It's hot in here. Well done Kimmy for putting on the heat,' Mum said.

I smirked at Carla.

'But, it was me!'

'Carla I don't care who it was. Will you go to the freezer and get a tub of colostrum and Kim can give the lamb a bottle when he's warm again?'

Carla paused for longer than was advisable.

'Stop day-dreaming and get a tub of colostrum.'

My sister approached the enormous chest freezer which was too big to be put into the kitchen so was sitting in the middle of the playroom. Carla was older and was able to lift the heavy lid of the newly purchased freezer, the like of which had never been seen before in Newtown House.

This freezer had the capacity to fit a baby elephant and was always overflowing with food. We were ready for a nuclear attack and had enough to feed the little village of Glencullen, where we lived. It was bursting at the seams with food from Ireland's much loved, good-value supermarket, Dunnes Stores. It contained St Bernard sliced-pans, St Bernard strawberry ice-cream, St Bernard frozen pizzas, St Bernard burgers, and a whole lot more including various cuts of meat.

When a lamb was slaughtered once a year, we would sit around the red Formica kitchen-table and Mum would fill freezer bags with cuts of lamb. My job was to label the bags, 'three lamb chops,' 'stewing lamb' or 'leg of lamb'.

The flow of red juices from the meat on the table enhanced the importance of our work and as I'd inhale the rank, fresh smell of flesh, I'd try hard to remind myself of how tasty next Sunday's dinner would be of succulent roast lamb and mint sauce. These precious zip-lock bags of lamb-cuttings would be carefully placed into the freezer to feed us throughout the winter, but in reality some might never be found again in that bottomless pit.

The colostrum milked from cows was frozen in old, disused yogurt-cartons and was an important nutritional substitute to feed baby lambs who were trying to stay alive for the first few hours of their lives.

St Bernard packaging in the baskets at the top of the freezer invariably hid any other produce which was hidden underneath and finding the colostrum was always going to be tricky.

Carla opened the freezer and the usual argument started.

'I can't find any in here.'

'What?' Mum roared back.

'Where is it?'

'It's in the left compartment.'

'Mum,' she bellowed, lifting her head out of the freezer, 'Is it under the cake-sponges or the frozen crispy-pancakes?'

'Oh, for God's sake, hurry up!'

'Found it. It was on top of the lamb shanks.'

Carla appeared with the recycled St. Bernard banana-flavoured yogurt carton, containing a frozen solidified liquid. She was wiping her nose with the back of her hand, which was now a reddish-blue colour, and she had frost shavings on her nose. None of this discomfort mattered, the mission was successfully completed.

My mother boiled the kettle and poured hot water into a bowl and the frozen tub bobbed on top of the water. She stopped in horror.

'I can't believe you! I asked you to do one simple job. Don't you know how busy we are? For crying out loud, this is an ice-pop Kim and Philip made yesterday from orange! Didn't you see the lollipop-stick plonked in the middle of it? Put the damn thing back and let Kim show you where to find the colostrum.'

208

I approached them to see what the commotion was about and what I could do to restore calm.

I was the peacemaker in the family. I found any kind of tension in the house unbearable and would try to diffuse tempestuous arguments (or silences) at all times. The lambing-period was the most stressful two months of the year and tiredness and worry can evoke many emotions in the most placid of families.

I did as I was told and handed Mum the correct tub. She made up the lamb's milk in an old Harp bottle, placed a baby's rubber teat over the mouth, handed it to me and returned to my Dad on the farm.

I squeezed some milk onto the lamb's nose and let it trickle down to his mouth. Then I placed the teat between his lips and he started to take little sups of milk. Very soon he began to suck the bottle with hungered enthusiasm.

As I felt the bottle being tugged from my hands and as the warm, yellow liquid leaked from his mouth through my fingers, I realised why there was so much fuss over this precious liquid. Colostrum was this lamb's life-line.

Formative years at school

1973

I COULDN'T wait to be part of an institution I knew I'd love. The first day of school couldn't come soon enough.

'I'm ready Mum! ' I yelled once again.

'Have you got your lunch-box?'

'Of course.'

'Good girl, into the car with the others and we'll go.'

Mum closed the front door and got into the car.

'Carla, where's your hockey stick?'

'Oh yeah. I'll get it now.'

'I have hers,' Ann said, before Carla had time to get out of the car.

'Now are you all sure you've everything?'

I hopped in between Ann, Carla and Philip. Mum turned on the engine and we started down the road towards the Montessori school, towards my new life.

The level of excitement in my chest was explosive when we pulled up outside the school. I looked up at the beautiful granite-faced-building, I beamed – here I was, Kim Maguire three-years-old and starting a sensational adventure.

Running up the steps ahead of Mum, I inhaled the unmistakable smell of crayons and books. It felt as though I'd come home. This was where I belonged.

'Come on,' I said, meandering through narrow corridors.

'I don't know why she's so excited,' Ann said demurely. 'It's just school.'

I ignored her. I was too engrossed in my own world and was running towards Miss Allen's room.

'Good morning Kim. Come in. Your place is at the table under the window.'

But I was already seated.

'Oh good girl you already know where to sit,' Miss Allen said, bending down to my height.

There was a frenzy of activity in the room with parents and children saying goodbye and mothers telling their children to mop up their tears. I, on the other hand, was hoping the adults would hurry up and leave.

The room was beautifully decorated with Montessori equipment. There were activity mats for us to sit on and I was devouring all I could see. I had a choice of activities, a brown stair to stack, a pink tower to build, and different sized cylindrical blocks to insert in round-shaped holes.

Suddenly I realised I was alone and started to feel afraid.

I want to go home. Where's my Mummy? I'm too little to be on my own.

A banging at the door and the sudden entrance of a habited nun made me jump.

'Good morning Miss Allen. Good morning children. You're all very welcome,' the smiling nun said, scanning the class. 'Now let's see who I already know. Yes I know Carla and Ann's sister, Kim.'

My cheeks reddened but I was happy by the attention.

My nervousness from this public recognition was short-lived, because I'd just laid eyes on some milk-bottles she was carrying. The bottles were fogged over from sitting in a cold fridge and the foil lids were indented from the nun's finger. She placed the bottles beside twenty-three cups and left the room.

Miss Allen requested everyone return to their places and put their lunchboxes on the table. My eyes grew bigger with excitement. I knew the drill: I'd sought the information from my sisters months before and had been practising 'snack time' with my teddies and three-limbed Tiny-Tears doll.

I waited for the next instruction.

'Now children will you open your lunchboxes.'

My little fingers moved swiftly and I ripped off the lid of my blue Tupperware lunchbox. I knew exactly what Mum had packed for me to eat and I removed the Clingfilm from two digestive biscuits. I sat haughtily with my snack in front of me and I watched other children struggling with Miss Allen's instructions and needing help to open their boxes. I nibbled the biscuits slowly – making sure I was being a good girl.

My first day and the following years at school were fantastic. I loved every aspect of school. I loved learning, I idolised my female teachers and most importantly, I was entering an exciting life which was unaffected by events on the farm. It didn't matter if there was rain and the hay couldn't be baled or weak lambs needed minding. The farm had no power over me at school. This was my escapism and brought me from my family's tomboy normality to soft, girly experiences. In school it was fine to be interested in dolls and prams and I could choose to play 'dress up' with my friends. School fulfilled the piece of me that I spent much of my early years fighting for.

April approached quickly and I started to get excited about my birthday. Mum threw wonderful birthday parties for my older sisters, younger brother and me. The girls and boys in my class were excited when they got invitations to the party. Even though it was during such a busy time on the farm, Mum kindly made golden Rice Crispie buns, chocolate-biscuit-cake, butterfly buns, fudge, jelly-tot marshmallows and much more. She made sandwiches and cooked cocktail-sausages. It was magical.

There was a buzz around the house when one of her children was having a party. The only child not to obey the 'wear old clothes' rule was me. I glided down the stairs in my best party dress which I'd only worn once to a party the previous month.

'You're not seriously going to wear your good maxi on the farm?' Mum denounced incredulously.

'Yep.'

She didn't look too happy so I altered my tone.

'Please I want to.'

'OK. But if you get it ruined, it's your fault and I won't be buying you another.'

I knew she meant what she said, but I didn't mind because the first of my friends had pulled into our driveway having successfully followed Mum's directions up the mountains, miles from suburbia.

'Come on lads into the trailer and we'll go on an adventure,' Dad said later in the afternoon. This was the pinnacle of the day. I'd experienced these thrills many times before at my sisters' parties.

'The tractor is over here,' I instructed my friends in a bossy voice. 'Get up onto the trailer.'

Dad put the lot of us onto his trailer and drove the tractor through the fields. He turned around, pretending he wasn't looking and aimed the tractor at a tree. It resembled a Christmas pantomime.

'Look in front of you Mr Maguire, you're going to crash. Watch out! Ah! There's a tree in front of the tractor!'

'Oh no there isn't!'

'Oh yes there is!' they retorted, terrified.

I knew he was only trick-acting and with that inside knowledge, I sat back laughing.

On and on the pantomime went. I'm not sure who got the most enjoyment from the game, my friends or Dad.

The following morning in school, I couldn't wait to hear the post-mortem – I knew the party was a success and I craved the attention which would ensue. My party was the talk of the school and my status grew.

Every year from then on, the chocolate-bar-bribery would start in March.

'If I give you this *Furry Friend* will you invite me to your party?'

Like chocolate, the power I had was addictive.

Then one day when I was eight, three girls from another class approached me.

'You're the one who lives on a farm, aren't you?' they sneered.

I nodded. They continued, 'Farms are disgusting. They're dirty and smelly. You smell of poo. Look everyone, Kim smells of cow poo!'

I froze.

I looked around for someone to help me but the girls were sniggering and were holding their fingers up to their noses. I shivered. I'd been found out. Tears started to well up in my eyes.

I want my big sisters.

The relationship between my home and school-life changed. They could no longer be integrated as one. I was the only girl in the school who was from a 'smelly' farm – there was nothing I could do to change that fact.

I went home and I cried all afternoon.

'Don't mind those girls, they're jealous of you. You're a big girl now and you tell them not to be so silly,' Mum said to me wiping my tears.

You don't understand. I hate the farm. I don't want to live here.

From then on I treated the farm (my parents' passion) as something to be ashamed of. I too started to repulse all things agricultural. If I wanted to fit in at school, I had to distance myself from my farming way of life.

'Come on for dinner everyone,' my mother shouted up the stairs to the others when she was finished comforting me.

Dad came into the kitchen just as my siblings came thundering down the stairs. We took our places at the table and Mum put our dinner in front of us.

I sat in between Philip and Ann on a bench opposite Mum and Dad, and Carla was at the top end. Steam was rising from our plates of roast chicken and vegetables. We were hungry after our day at school and we wanted to eat.

Mum started the mealtime ritual.

'Bless yourselves. In the Name of the Father, Ann don't even think of lifting your fork, and of the Son and of the Holy Spirit...' I put down my knife and joined in. When the prayer-before-meals was over, Dad put the wireless on.

Oh no, bad timing!

The six o'clock Angelus-dong blasted from the speaker and we were obliged to re-place our cutlery on our plates and regretfully mumble the responses to a prayer we wouldn't have understood even if we had known the correct words. We hummed along and sporadically threw out random responses: 'and dealt amungus', or something similar.

Eventually we picked up our cutlery and started to eat the luke-warm dinner.

'I got a sweet in school today,' I said proudly, eating my dinner.

'Well done love, that's great,' Mum said, gesturing to Dad to turn down the radio.

'No, shush, the news is on.'

Our cue to be silent.

'Kim and Philip stop messing. Kim, I won't tell you again!'

The news was followed by the sports' results. Eventually the volume of the radio was turned down and we chatted as a family until the Farming Programme came on at 6.20 p.m. The volume was put up even louder than before and I heard something resembling, 'In Blessingtown Market today, ewes started at £38, black-faced hoggets at £42 and lambs went for 87p a pound.'

'Give that back,' Carla growled at Ann. 'Mum, she's taken my knife.'

Mum gave Ann a look.

Ann threw the knife onto Carla's plate, hitting it more forcefully than she'd anticipated.

We all looked at Dad.

'STOP it for God's sake!'

Silence.

The Farming Programme continued without further incident, until the news started again at 6.30 p.m.

Mum had insisted we would never have the TV in our kitchen as it was our time to share stories of the happenings of the day, but in reality there was so much shushing and giving out that the imposition of a TV would have paled into significance. Between 6 and 6.40 p.m., the wireless was king.

I was often reminded by Mum, that like it or not, farming was who we were and I needed to be respectful of my roots. Of course my parents were right and I am embarrassed I was an ungrateful, moody teenager. My parents worked hard to give us the best and all I did was ridicule. They were generous, loving, caring and hard-working. Unselfishly they put me through school and in later years, teacher-training college. But sometimes I just couldn't help myself. I had turned into a complete snob.

Reunion with Melissa

2009

MY sadness pulled me back into the present in the NRH. Nostalgia was taking over and I needed a stimulant to pick me up. Like an addict I wanted a hit – I was going cold turkey. My drug wasn't an illegal vice like cocaine or heroin but rather an overwhelming need to tell my story. I looked around for some prey and I wasn't disappointed. A new shipment of patients had arrived and my heart was beating a little faster. The drug would be pulsing through my veins soon. I wandered out of the room and approached a potential victim. My opening words,

'Hi, do you mind if I sit down?'

'Yeah sure. No problem'.

'You've had a stroke too?' I asked.

'That's right. I live in Castletown, you know where it is? It's five miles from Jonestown. Well, there I was gardening and all of a sudden I collapsed. My wife arrived. I'm sure you know her, she's always in and out to see me. Well she got such a fright when the rake was lying in the flowerbed. I was planting winter pansies and pruning rose bushes...'

OK, it's time to change tactic. I'll not get a hit from this middle-aged man. He's not letting me talk and is actually preying on me.

Over the years I had learned to invite others into conversations by questioning them about their welfare and interests. Unfortunately I wasn't adept at opening conversations by talking about myself but if I didn't learn quickly, I'd have the DTs. Less egotistical stroke survivors, who might give me some space to talk and off-load, were what I needed.

We all had our own story. Everyone's story was shocking in its own way, but each of us was alone in our anguish. We shared similarities and tried to form friendships in the atypical environment of the rehabilitation hospital. But it was no good. We had been randomly thrown together into an institution and whilst we had all suffered a traumatic event, we'd little else in common outside of this. We were too different and were frenziedly trying to cope. My family and friends had to become the cochlear implants I so desperately needed.

I returned to the communal room deflated – I hadn't found anyone to talk to. However, my spirits lifted when I looked up and saw a pudgy face peeking out of a white crochet blanket.

'Hi!' I called to Kieran as he strolled towards me with Dylan in his arms. I embraced them simultaneously.

'Excellent timing. Hi Mr Gorgeous, how are you doing my cute little boy? Hi Kieran, how are you? How's Dylan? How's he feeding?'

'He's a hungry buster and wolfs bottles down. He's like your side of the family, the way he loves his grub.'

'That's great to hear. I miss him so much. How he's doing?'

We sat on chairs beside the windows on the corridor where only ten minutes ago I'd been searching for someone to listen to me.

'I'm getting a chill,' I said. 'Come on, let's go upstairs to my room. It's too cold for Dylan and me.'

We got the lift up to my floor and when Kieran opened my bedroom door, the heat coming from the radiator hit us. Kieran placed Dylan on my bed and tried to open the window.

I sat beside Dylan and I started to take off his anorak. I could feel the heat of his body.

'I want to feed him,' I said looking at the formula powder and a bottle of sterile water peeping out of the baby-bag.

I placed the bottle between my knees and with one hand I tried to pour the powder into the bottle but most of it fell on the floor.

'I'll do it,' Kieran said, starting to make up a second bottle.

Silence.

I was upset that I couldn't feed my baby independently and Kieran was annoyed with the whole situation. It was my fault I spilled the powder – me who was causing Kieran's fury.

Keeping Kieran from being angry had been foremost on my mind since my stroke. If he got angry where would that leave me? I relied on him so much. He helped me dress, he planned for our future, and sometimes he was both mother and father to our baby.

I took the bottle from Kieran and I looked at Dylan who was now propped up on two of my pillows. I placed the bottle in his mouth and he began to suck just like the baby lambs did when

I used to feed them colostrum as a child. My breathing resembled my thought process. The in-breath took in the beauty of my child, and my out-breath released the sadness I was feeling. The whole experience was surreal and I wondered when I would wake from the numbness. A sudden knock on the door made me jump.

'Melissa! Hi. Oh my God!' I spluttered, breaking down in tears when I saw my best friend at the door.

'Hi Kim and Kieran.'

We embraced for a very long time and the two of us sobbed. It was a reunion of two souls. It was a physical, spiritual and an emotional unification all at the same time and injected me with strength, giving me permission to drop my defences, open my heart and bare my soul.

'Melissa, what happened to me?' I beseechingly asked my confidante, my supporter.

'I don't know.'

'What happened? What happened?'

I could hold it in no longer. The same sound, which I had once emitted four years before when I heard I had miscarried, came screeching from somewhere deep down. The sound frightened me and I looked over at Dylan, silently apologising to him for expressing such grief in his presence. Melissa looked at him too and tickled his little toes.

'This is Dylan,' I said mustering up pride and wiping my tears away.

She gazed at him and then at me and she embraced me even tighter. She had known how much we wanted a family and had been really pleased when I announced I was pregnant.

'Kieran, he's gorgeous.'

Melissa and he hugged each other tightly, offering each other solace.

'Thanks.'

Kieran took his leave and headed away with Dylan in his arms. All I could see was the hood of Dylan's blue anorak as he was returned to his temporary home with my family in Glencullen.

'Sit down,' I said.

Melissa and I sat beside each other on my bed in silence. I needed to tell her everything. I needed her to know what I was going through.

But she already knew.

She recognised pain and we knew each other long enough to know when our sadness outweighed our joy.

'My heart's broken Melissa, it's broken in half.'

'I know it is.'

'Why. Oh why? I did everything right and everything was taken from me.'

I didn't need to explain to her that I was talking about the pregnancy and the care I took looking after both Dylan's and my health throughout the nine months.

'Maybe that's what stood to you. Maybe that's why you both survived. You gave him life by all you did. You ensured he'd live.'

Oh, wise one.

I missed Melissa when she left later. It was my first night in the NRH and I was alone once more.

First day in the NRH

'ARE you awake?' a Filipino nurse asked me when she entered the door the following morning.

I had always been an early riser and during the night of artificial heating and subsequent bed sweats, I had been awake since 5 a.m. and was waiting for someone to come and get me out of bed and tell me what to do.

'You like shower?'

'Thank you for being so kind to me last night.'

'You welcome. This happens to some patients – they get upset in the night. But you OK now?'

I nodded.

'Sit down on the wheelchair, I bring you to shower. Where is your towel and soap? Ready, we must go through the man's ward.'

Some of the curtains were drawn around beds and there was plenty of activity in the ward. I didn't know where to look when I was wheeled past beds with men of various ages who were in different states of undress. I lowered my head in vain pretence I wasn't an intruder trespassing in their lives, or I wasn't taking in the demeaning indecency of their situation.

The showering situation in this hospital in 2010 seemed as though it were something from the last century. Cleaning trolleys had to be removed from the shower-room and I sat in disbelief at the very basic facilities I was being exposed to in an Irish hospital. As much as I tried, I couldn't but compare the hospital to those in Cyprus and I was embarrassed for Ireland.

I struggled in the shower. I found it hard to undress and the small distance I'd to walk from the chair to the shower was daunting as I wasn't able to hold onto a handrail and I was afraid I'd fall.

My dressing-gown and pyjamas, wet from my ineffective use of the shower-head, were too damp to put on. A nurse came in and said she'd dress me when I got back to my room. I nodded in agreement. I sat in the chair naked and she placed two towels over me, attempting to protect my modesty. I was wheeled back through the men's ward, feeling low and exposed. Humiliation and lack of self-worth are difficult emotions to deal with, but I was nearly past caring.

The nurse brought me back to my room. I was dressed, and I eventually escaped down the lift to the dining room for breakfast.

A clattering and banging of catering equipment reverberated through the corridors on the ground floor in the conservatory area. Mealtimes in the NRH were nice little periods of escapism. I queued behind a young man, Charles, who told me he had lost his legs due to diabetes. I followed him into the restaurant, watched as he pushed his tray along the metal rails at the food counter and asked the smiling restaurant staff-member for porridge and toast. Then, placing his tray on his lap, he wheeled himself to a table to eat.

Tending to observe etiquette before jumping in, I copied Charles' actions, shared some morning pleasantries with the same staff member and put my sweet porridge and tea-pot onto my tray. I looked on helplessly – I'd no spare hand to carry my tray. Using my stick to walk was still a necessity for me and anyway carrying a heavy tray with one hand would most certainly have caused a hot-tea scalding of some sort.

But the catering staff understood the needs of the hemiplegic patient and without me asking, a woman brought my tray over to the dining-table.

'What's your first therapy today?' Charles asked me when I sat down beside him.

'I've physiotherapy later, but first I want to take a little walk around to get my bearings.'

When I'd finished breakfast, I strolled along the corridors on my own. I walked towards the sports' hall and looked at the names of the departments I was passing.

The Occupational Therapy Department was to my right and then looking left I saw it: a school! Our Lady of Lourdes Primary School for children who were attending the hospital. This was my area of expertise. I shouldn't be ambling corridors as a patient: I should be teaching. I'd go in there later to let the teachers and principal know I was more than just a debilitated woman – I was a professional in the field of education. I had secured a first class honours degree in a Masters of Education. I was first and foremost a teacher.

Nobody should be complacent. A stroke could happen to anyone, even a professional. What's my baby doing at the moment?

I put my sadness aside and went to find the physiotherapy room.

Automatic doors opened, announcing my entrance to my long-anticipated physiotherapy session. I looked meekly around the huge sport's hall. I approached a fresh-faced physiotherapist and explained who I was.

'I'll see who'll be working with you. Take a seat here,' she said, offering a hand to help me sit down on a long blue plinth close to where I was standing.

I put my hand on the plinth, sat and was grateful for the rest. My hip and posterior were hurting from all of the walking I had been doing and I needed a break.

The large wooden-floored room was divided in half: spinal injuries in the upper half and acquired brain injuries the lower. Sizeable windows illuminated the work-space and as I looked out, I noticed dark clouds hovering over the hospital. I thought of home and how the weather was always worse in the Dublin Mountains, which were 1,000 feet higher than Dun Laoghaire. Was it snowing at home? More importantly, would Kieran and Dylan be able to make it down to me safely?

Recent graduates seemed to make up a moderate portion of physiotherapists working in the room. I had always assumed that physiotherapists in the NRH were employed after being hand-picked by the hospital for their experience. But looking at the young faces, I had to revisit my previous assumptions. I wasn't sure if I'd been quite right. In my revised opinion, I guessed some of the young physiotherapists were in fact gaining experience in rehabilitation.

Had these young physiotherapists been specifically employed because of their expertly-acquired experience working in this specialist field? I didn't know, and I didn't know if my expectations were too high. I wasn't looking for youth, I was looking for experience, which many new graduates wouldn't have. Searching for something I couldn't find, I was beginning to resent those around me who were too young and speciously inexperienced to have the capacity to cure me.

'Hi Kim, I'm Shauna, your physiotherapist,' a young woman said pleasantly.

'Hi.'

She's only a fledgling. I should be at home with Dylan.

'Let me take a look at your upper limb. Would you mind lying down and I'll examine the range in your arm. Do you have any pain in your shoulder?'

'Yes I do.'

She reached for my arm. Her red hair fell across one of her shoulders and I'd to close my eye as I felt strands of her hair fall onto my face. Long, beautiful hair smelling of lemon teased me as it contrasted my short, boyish hair.

Lifting my affected arm, to check the range in my shoulder, Shauna slowly pulled it up behind my head and then out to the side. I squealed in pain when my arm had reached its optimum limit.

'Well done, that's not too bad. Now let me take a look at your hand.'

My fingers were curled into the palm of my hand and Shauna gently pulled them open.

'Does that hurt?' she asked.

'No not at all.'

'You're lucky you don't have too much tone or spasticity in your upper limb. We'll get a resting orthotic made for you which you can wear in bed or watching TV. It will keep your fingers looser and your nails won't dig into the palm of your hand. Throughout your time here, I'll stretch your fingers, your arm and keep movement in your scapula. The overall objective will be for you to be able to use your left arm as a weight to secure things. For example when you're writing, your left arm will prevent the paper from moving.'

Her words made me sit up sluggishly – almost in slow motion.

'You mean, you don't think I'll get any function in it again?'

Shauna looked at me in an apologetic way.

'I can't say for sure. We'll have to wait and see what happens.'

But no matter how she dressed it up, I sensed the truth had been released. Neither Andry, Kostas nor Shauna carried the belief I would have two working hands. Their professionalism had taught them not to be overly honest with a patient and to allow the patient hold onto some hope, but I knew what they were thinking.

I'll show them. I'll be a medical miracle.

Then looking at my tripod stick, she asked,

'Can you walk?'

I nodded.

'Will you be able to walk up the hall for me?'

I stood up from the plinth and she held my elbow to assist me. I tried to put one leg in front of the other and wobbled as I took my first demonstrative steps for her.

Embarrassment predominated when I was performing this meagre exercise in the large hall. I felt there were eyes on me as I leant helplessly on my stick and circumvented my left leg in a semi-circle ensuring I didn't trip over my dropped-foot. There may have been up to twenty people working in the room and in reality there were very few eyes on me but *my* eyes were on me.

I watched Shauna's reaction to see if there was any sign of hope etched on her face. Had she additional knowledge which Andry and Kostas hadn't? Maybe she could see potential for a full recovery? But her demeanour told me nothing.

'I want to get advice on an orthotic for you. It would help you walk more effectively.'

Another orthotic. My heart's aching here, in the NRH without my son.

I sat down on the plinth again feeling somewhat deflated. A lower-limb brace didn't sound hopeful to me.

The orthotist was already in the hall and Shauna called him over. He smiled at me and chatted kindly before Shauna and he examined my walk. I paraded up and down in front of them for what seemed like an endless amount of time. They were looking at my gait, and muscle function. I wanted them to look at me and not my disability. I was a person first and my disability was second. Ultimately this exercise was for my benefit, but their analytic whispering was upsetting. After some time Shauna said,

'You did very well. I know it's not easy when we are studying every step you take. You're doing great and once you have your new orthotic you can stop using your stick.'

She's kind, she's good, there's hope.

'This is the end of your session. I'll see you tomorrow at 3 p.m.'

I got up to leave and walked towards a door at the top of the hall where I'd seen patients enter and exit but Shauna shouted after me,

'Please don't use that door, it's for the staff.'

My face was slapped by this unnecessary comment and I felt I was a three-year-old being chastised by my mother. A door was a door and did it matter which door staff or patients used? My lack of self-confidence, insecurity and shame were being used as a whipping-stick by this young woman and the rage inside me started to build for the first time since my stroke. I would choose whichever bloody door suited me.

Fury concealed my vulnerability. I had survived a brain haemorrhage and I was mourning my lost body. She was young and invincible. In that sentence, she'd shown little respect for the person, for my illness or my fragility.

How dare she? I want to go home. I want to turn back the clock.

Many patients were going through a huge upheaval in their lives and needed compassion. My studies had given me a heighted awareness of the basic human need for acceptance. But I had never practised as a psychotherapist: I didn't know how difficult it must have been for anyone working with emotive patients like me. However, I had been a teacher for years, had a lot of experience working with children with special educational needs and I knew the level of empathy which needs to be shown. Credence in a person with or without a disability is paramount for any kind of therapist to have. Perhaps a lack of life-experience does not quite equip a person in the emotional perplexity of rehabilitation.

In hindsight, I now ask myself was my blaming of others to do with my waning hope, and was I projecting this desperation onto those who couldn't cure me? I was being unfair and ungrateful: maybe it was I who wasn't self-accepting or empathetic of my own injury.

I walked out of the sport's hall with my head slumped and headed towards the dining-room where a queue of people in wheelchairs was lined up outside the door. A smell of bacon wafted through the corridors and was comparable to dinner-times in the boarding school I attended for a year when I was twelve-years-old. Back then we were always hungry at dinner times. We would push and shove one another as we queued, inhaling the predictable day's meal of beef stew, chicken pie or bacon and cabbage.

Today as an adult, I wasn't comfortable joining the dinner queue I had so readily joined as a youngster; besides I was in too much pain to stand.

Soon the canteen doors were unlocked and the queue shortened. I was no longer the same novice as I had been that morning and I started the process of ordering dinner. I knew where the trays were, I knew what was on the menu and I knew how helpful the canteen staff would be.

Even though my emotional hunger was still very prevalent, my bodily appetite had not returned to any great extent. With a yogurt and a slice of bacon on my tray, I sat down beside Charles and two women I had noticed at breakfast. My physiotherapy session had left me exposed – I needed kind-heartedness from someone.

'Hi, how's your morning been?' Charles asked warmly.

'Good,' I lied.

'You'll get the hang of things soon enough. Can I ask you what happened when you had your stroke?'

The women looked up from their dinners and the three of them listened to my story, showing concern and interjecting at appropriate times. Their kindness restored my former trust in people and I felt better in myself. I'd got my fix for the day.

'See you later,' I shouted back to them when I got up from the table to go to my final therapy. Looking at my timetable, I saw the words occupational therapy.

I wonder what will that entail?

My sister Carla had trained as an occupational therapist in the college which was on the same grounds in the NRH, twenty-five years ago. Did I really know anything about her old career? Geriatrics, disabilities, and preparation for independent living were the only things I could remember her ever talking about and I currently I fitted into two of those categories.

Who would have thought I'd be a patient of one of her peers? What will they do to me?

Emotional recovery

'HI Kim, I'm Ava. You're really welcome. Why don't you come this way and we'll have a chat?'

From the word go, my occupational therapist, Ava, filled me with trust and admiration. She was vibrant and lovely, empathetic and enthusiastic.

Ava spent a considerable amount of time chatting to me and taking notes. I sat back thinking I'd enjoy the sessions with her until she dropped a bomb-shell.

'We're going down to Superquinn in Blackrock to do some shopping today.'

Blackrock, of all places! Say if I bump into somebody I know?

But I wasn't going to back out. I'd do anything to accelerate my recovery. I followed Ava down the corridor towards the back doors of the hospital.

A blue transit van reversed towards the door and four other patients and I waited as a hydraulic lift to the rear of the van, was lowered. We took it in turns to stand on the metal grate. The lift heightened and we got into the back of the van.

I felt humiliated.

Not another feeling of shame to be endured. Wasn't it bad enough being on a hydraulic lift getting onto the plane in Larnaca? Surely I can manage to get into this van through the doors and not through the rear.

236

But I said nothing and did what I was told. The next time I knew I'd speak up and explain that with a little help I should be able to get into the van the usual way. And that's exactly what I did. Problem solved!

Yellow lights on Christmas trees were glistening in houses and I felt melancholic. The van was travelling through traffic in the Southside of Dublin – an area I used to know so well as a teenager but hadn't visited for many years.

Stradbrook Rugby Club had been the pinnacle of my social life at one stage. My friends and I used to go to the disco there on Saturday nights: hunting. We were rarely disappointed. Before leaving our respective homes, caked in make-up and cheap eye-shadow, we'd smuggle small bottles of vodka (stolen from our parents' drinks' cabinets) past the not-so-burly bouncers at the door of the club, and then add the precious spirits to glasses of cider or beer. It was the first establishment we went to which served alcohol, and although we were only seventeen-years-old, bottles of Stag and Budweiser mixed with large measures of vodka were consumed with vigour; increasing confidence in our quest for a 'snog'! We were on top of the world.

Twenty-five years on, I was now in a van being driven past this great memory after fulfilling all of my childhood dreams: becoming a teacher, getting married, and having a child. Serious illness had not been part of the grand plan.

We arrived into the car park in Superquinn and we got out of the van.

Christmas decorations draped from the ceiling in Blackrock Shopping Centre. It was approaching 3 p.m. and the lights were on in the shops. 'Oh Holy Night' played from loudspeakers and I tried to shut out the haunting voice of the soprano, endeavouring to block the imminent emotion which was sure to ensue from hearing my favourite Christmas carol.

'I've a list here of items I'd like you to find in the supermarket,' Ava said to the five of us who had gathered around her at the trolley-collection point.

I took the list and wondered how I'd manage the task.

Pushing a trolley with one hand takes some expertise, and after overturning a display of Christmas cards, and walking away indignantly as though it were the shop's fault for placing them at the end of an aisle, I learned that if I pushed my trolley forward a little and then pulled it from the front, I could navigate through the supermarket. I filled my trolley with the required items and gleamed with pride when I was first to have successfully completed this task – ever the competitor.

The success of this shopping trip was unexpectedly satisfying because it meant that in the future, when I needed groceries, I'd be able to do it, and this task became an encouraging moment for me.

There was hope out there. I only needed to let it in. But I was afraid. To let in hope, meant acceptance and I would never accept what happened to me, Kieran and Dylan at such an important time in our lives.

'Hi Ava,' I said with a smile when I met the following day in the Occupational Therapy Department.

We were standing outside a little integrated-kitchen which was used to encourage domesticity and to prepare patients for their return home.

'Come on into our kitchen and you can make scones,' Ava said to me.

How can somebody with no function in one arm possibly be able to bake?

There was no time for discussion. Ava handed me a recipe.

'This kitchen resembles ordinary kitchens in homes in Ireland. It's up to you to find the ingredients and utensils in the presses. You will need to reach, to bend and be creative making these scones.'

I looked at her, seriously baffled.

'I'll be here if you need help. You're well able to do this.'

Encouraging independence helped me more than anything. Various plastic mats were available to me to steady the mixing-bowl and when I cut the mixture into circles, Ava looked on as I placed the scones onto tins and put them in the oven.

'Now, let's do the washing up.'

My legs were getting weak as I had been standing for more than twenty minutes but the belief she had in me gave me the confidence to go to the sink, turn on the tap and fill the basin with hot water and washing-up liquid. The smell of scones baking was the nicest smell I'd experienced in quite some time. I was the creator of this aroma and it felt good. It was Ava who convinced me to return to cooking dinners and baking (a passion of mine learned from the master-baker – Mum).

Ava and the other occupational therapists in the NRH had very practical plans in place for their patients' return home. A type of normality prevailed in their kitchen when I was cooking or stacking the dishwasher. I was achieving much more than I thought possible and I was proud of myself. I had hope that I could deal with my new situation if no function ever returned in my arm.

I linked my arm into Kieran's and we went down to the coffee-shop.

Blue floor tiles reflected light from ceiling lights, making the shop look a little bigger than it actually was. Two fridges with drinks and sandwiches, three circular tables and a counter were all that was in this small area. I liked going there. Patients were treated as people and weren't segregated because of a disability. Visitors, staff and patients were equal.

'Do you see her over there?' I whispered to Kieran when we were seated.

True to his profession, he covertly surveyed the room and nodded at me.

I explained, 'She was here yesterday. She's the parent of a child I used to teach.'

The stylish woman, sporting perfect red lipstick and wearing knee-high boots got up from her chair to leave and without hesitating, I called her name. She turned to look at me and approached smiling. Her warmth and acceptance had momentarily made me forget my shame and my stroke. I had been her daughter's teacher for two years and the conversation we embarked upon was a typical teacher/parent chat about her daughter. What was she doing now? Was she in college?

When I'd first noticed the woman the previous day, her glamour and poise had made me turn away in case she was shocked by the unstylish me. Perhaps it was due to the little spark of hope I had experienced with Ava in the Occupational Therapy Room, but I was feeling confident, and gave myself permission to be seen by somebody from the past. It felt good to invite compassionate energy into my life and I was proud I had instigated this unexpected reunion.

In those few minutes I felt seen. My past, which I was so fervently afraid of, was slowly integrating into the present. Unknown to her, her kindness and approval helped me on my journey of self-acceptance.

'Kieran, I think I am going to text a few old friends to see if they'd like to come to see me.'

'Are you ready?'

'I think so. I'll chat with the psychologist when I see her soon. She might prepare me for what's to come.'

'I'm really happy for you.'

'Thanks Kieran, you're always a great support and I appreciate your words of encouragement.'

We grinned at each other and played with Dylan's fingers.

'I suppose we'd better go and let you find the psychologist for your appointment.'

'See you later for our date.'

Rehabilitating to go home

I FOUND the psychologist's office with little difficulty, knocked on the door and waited to be invited in. I knew I needed her council and hoped this woman would be able to offer me some.

'Come on in and take a seat over there,' she said, pointing to a chair to the side of her desk. I did as I was told and waited for her to open a new manila file for me – her patient. An impression of her was already forming in my mind. She was gentle but professional. A woman of small stature with brown hair and a caring face, she reminded me of one of my old school friends. We were of similar age and under different circumstances, we could perhaps have been friends.

'Welcome Kim,' she began, 'I'm Sharon. How are you finding things here?' she asked, placing the empty file on the table.

'Fine.'

'You've been through a lot. Would you like to tell me about it?'

Words began to slobber out of my mouth. She looked, she listened, and didn't interrupt. Sharon was everything I had been taught a therapist could be and I felt safe in her capable hands. I was vindicated at last – she recognised all my symptoms of grief. I finished my story and we started to chat about my brain injury.

'Cognitively preserved' was one of the diagnosis I had once overheard a doctor say, and I light-heartedly told her this. For me the preservation of my cognition and intellect, speech and understanding, were paramount. It frightened me that if anyone thought my intelligence was compromised, I'd be treated differently.

Some weeks later, when my grief wasn't quite as raw, Sharon suggested we would do some psychological assessments. The assessments were somewhat similar to some of the assessments I used to carry out on the children in my school. Spatial reasoning, spatial awareness, word recognition, comprehension and problem-solving: the list went on. Being the recipient of testing, rather than the assessor was mortifying, but it made me think of how children may have felt during my assessment of them, and I was both humbled and embarrassed by the experience.

My time spent with Sharon was of immense help and I am indebted to her, as a therapist, for wiping my tears and for leaving her official psychologist-hat in the manila file.

The lighting in the pub was low, which showed off the bar's contemporary décor. Kieran and I sat at a round table and were handed bar menus. It was Thursday night; our date night, when we went out for a meal together in Dun Laorghaire. I hadn't got dressed up. I wasn't wearing mascara. My footwear wasn't elongating my legs. Three sprays of Coco Chanel hadn't left a trail in the air and my black tracksuit bottoms didn't resemble anything I'd worn on a date before. But I was happy to be out with Kieran.

Kieran was his usual handsome self. How I longed to be his visual equal with an able body. What would people think if they saw us together as a couple? I was pretty sure no one would think we were life-long partners. A partnership is usually the coming together of people with similarities but to all intents and purposes, there were few physical likenesses.

For his part, Kieran kept telling me how proud he was of me and how grateful he and Dylan were that I'd stayed alive for them. He reminded me I was beautiful and courageous. He said he respected me more than anyone he'd ever known and always held his head up high when we were in public together.

'I texted two of my friends today and they're coming to see me on Tuesday. The psychologist and I discussed the pros and cons, and I'm happy to see them as I know they'll really listen. Good friends who care are what I need at the moment.'

'I think that's really brave of you Kim. One step at a time. You're amazing! Do you want me to be with you when they visit?'

'No, I'd like to do this on my own. I've told them to meet me downstairs at the coffee-shop. I know it'll be fine.'

'Good. What was physiotherapy like today?'

'Actually, it went well. She did some arm and leg exercises which Kostas used to do and she had me walking up and down the hall with the new orthotic on my leg. She thinks I won't need a walking stick. Of course that terrifies me, but there are rails along the corridors and I can hold onto them until I'm steadier on my feet.'

I lifted my tracksuit bottom to show him the new ankle-foot-orthotic (AFO) which was like an open ski boot make of hard plastic and was strapped across my left leg and foot.

'We'll have to find some shoes the orthotic will fit into. Will you ask her has she any idea where to go? It looks very big. Your shoes might need to be two sizes bigger than you really are to accommodate it.'

'This is nice. It feels nice being here with you. It feels normal.'

Kieran held my hand over the table and looked into my eyes.

'Yes, it is nice. I love you and Dylan loves his Mummy. Life would be very different, empty, and worthless if I didn't have the two of you.'

For the first time in months, I tried to put myself into Kieran's shoes and I believed what he said. His life would have altered significantly had I not survived. He looked at me again.

'Why don't you stay in your Mum's house, instead of the hospital, and I can bring you down to the NRH each morning?'

'I feel safe staying in the hospital and having my day mapped out for me. Besides, the snow is so bad in Glencullen we mightn't be able to get down to Dun Laoghaire in the mornings. The hospital is warm and I need to stay warm. You know how cold my left side gets.'

'But I don't understand. Why won't you stay with us?'

No one could possibly understand. I couldn't live with my parents and family, pretending things were normal and unchanged. I didn't want to be faced with my disability in a house where for years, I hadn't had a disability. I needed to be sheltered in hospital, rehabilitating at my own pace without family monitoring my every move.

'I'm not ready yet.'

'That's fine Kim, but we're going home to Killaloe for the weekend, aren't we?'

I nodded in agreement.

'Dylan and I will collect you at lunchtime tomorrow and we'll go back home for two nights.'

Part
Four

A new life in Ballina-Killaloe

A COLD sunny day in February marked the end of my institutional life. We were leaving Dublin behind, and everywhere I looked there were cars speeding either side of us on the main Dublin-Limerick road, full of people going about their business. I was no longer in the hands of others.

This was not our first time to return home and during the previous weekend visits, our house had seemed different. It was bigger than I'd remembered, more beautiful but grossly inadequate in its ability to make me think things hadn't changed. Six weeks previously, when I'd first opened the front door and stepped into the hall, I had looked up the stairs where a newly installed banister had screamed 'disability' at me. It hadn't been there when I'd left the house a year and a half before. It was on the wall opposite the other one and I'd have to hold it so I could drag my leg up each step of the stairs to the first floor into the sanctuary of my bedroom.

I hadn't slept in that sanctuary during those few brief weekends when we had stayed over, because the good memories I'd had from eight wonderful years sleeping there with Kieran were difficult to deal with. Insulating myself from the world, I had slept downstairs in the guest room. I needed to be alone. The spare bedroom held no affinity for me – I'd no memories of having slept there as an able-bodied person. It was uninviting, plainly decorated and I wanted to hide away in it – I felt I deserved this demotion of sorts.

But things were beginning to change. We were home for good.

'Don't even think you're sleeping in there,' Kieran said, as I looked into the spare room. 'It's time for us to start to bring some semblance of normality back to our lives. You're able to go upstairs, so please sleep up there with me.'

My lover of eighteen years was now asking me to return to our marital bed which in itself posed many difficulties. I was different from before, my body had changed. How could I possibly be attractive to him when I couldn't bear to look at my own reflection in the mirror? Kieran was asking too much of me: the time wasn't right yet and I ignored his words 'bringing a semblance of normality back to our lives.' The disdain I had for my body was stronger than his love for it. I wanted to sleep alone where he couldn't see me.

So I made up an excuse.

'But you won't be able to sleep in the bed with me. My leg spasms during the night and I'll keep you awake.'

'I don't care. Dylan and I need you with us. We're a family and I think the three of us should share the same room. Dylan's six-months-old and we won't get this time back.'

I knew only too well I'd never get this time back. I wanted to press pause on Dylan's development but he just kept growing and moving ahead.

Slow down baby Dylan; wait for me.

Reluctantly I went up the stairs to our bedroom. Kieran was ahead of me and pushed the door open, stood back and let me walk in. I looked around the room and taking it all in – the cream carpet, the king-size bed, the mahogany drawers and Dylan's cot – I wondered where it all went wrong. I walked past the bed towards the balcony door and stared out over the river Shannon flowing carelessly past Kincora towards the bridge in Killaloe. I wished I was back in my old life – a life which had flowed so effortlessly like the Shannon.

I turned my head despondently and peeked into the ensuite bathroom and noticed that everything we had sent home from Cyprus had been returned to shelves and drawers in the bathroom.

'Who did all this?' I inquired. 'Who unpacked our things and put everything away?'

'They kept coming. Our friends kept coming that day. They gave their time, their support and help for a full day. I couldn't believe how good they were and what kind friends we have. Kim, they're all so concerned for you and for us. Each plastic container full of clothes and toiletries was emptied and the contents returned to wardrobes and drawers. All of the boxes you had put into the attic are now empty and, because you were so organised before Cyprus by labelling each one, it made finding linen and towels for all of the rooms much easier.'

'That was nice of them.'

It was lovely hearing Kieran speak of that day in early December when ten of our close friends gave up their Saturday to offer Kieran the practical support he needed. They got our house ready, enabling us to return to a clean and organised home. No one had questioned him when he sought their assistance – they all wanted to help in some way, and they did.

I was touched by what they had done but the realisation of people going through my possessions was something I hadn't thought about up to this point.

'It should have been me sorting it out. I wanted to do that; it's my house,' I blubbered. 'They were my things: my sheets, my personal diaries, my tampons. I wanted to do it.'

'I know,' he said with feeling.

'They were all great, but it was my job, a job I couldn't do and it's not fair.'

'I know.'

'I always wanted to sort out Dylan's clothes and fold them neatly into drawers. I've waited so long to rub his babygros on my cheek and inhale the smell of fabric softener. I was robbed of it. It's not right, he's my son and I wasn't able to do basic things for him. Why?'

I couldn't speak any more. This was still the unanswerable question. Why? No one was able to find answers to the whys. Why did it happen? Why was God so cruel? Why me?

Now I wanted to sleep downstairs in the impersonal setting of the guest room: a room untouched by others' hands.

As it turned out, even if I'd wanted to stay in the downstairs' bedroom, I couldn't because we needed the room for an au pair.

A week after our return home to Ballina, Kieran had to go back to work on a full-time basis. His work colleagues and managers had been more than understanding and had facilitated him when he sought time off. They had covered his workload without complaint and had even donated some of their overtime hours to him. Like my teaching staff, they had also helped us out financially. We were indebted to so many.

But I wouldn't be able to manage on my own and I needed live-in help.

Don't leave me alone

MUM arrived to our house the next day to help us out. It was Saturday and Kieran wanted to do some work on his boat, *Sophie*. The boat was his pride and joy and he'd talked incessantly about sailing during the time we'd been abroad.

When Kieran had bought *Sophie* years before, he had gone to the AIB in Limerick city and had withdrawn wads of sterling. He had walked up O'Connell Street, £50 notes stuffed in all his pockets. He'd hopped into a taxi and had gone to Shannon airport. Going through customs without a care in the world, whilst smuggling a substantial amount of money out of the country to the UK, hadn't fazed him at all. He'd paid for *Sophie* in cash, sailed her to Kinsale where I'd inspected our investment. It had been was worth every penny. She was ours to keep.

But *Sophie* was his now. I'd no interest in her anymore. He was her sole owner. My 'deck-boy' title was lost and I could never see myself reefing sails, tying warps or making dinners for us following long days on the water. The wonderful times spent together out on the lake and chartering boats in Croatia were to be no more. I couldn't even get onto the damn thing. I resented every inch of the boat as it represented things I could no longer do.

'I'm going to *Sophie* for a while,' Kieran said to me, packing the car with paintbrushes and tins of anti-fouling paint.

Kieran was leaving me behind with my mother so he could be alone and get lost in his own world. It was hard for me to watch him escape from all that was going on. I pretended I didn't mind him going and got engrossed in a conversation with Mum.

My self-obsession and lengthy explanations of all I was going through must have been tiresome and upsetting for a mother to hear day after day. The conversations were mostly one way. I still had little interest in what people said, unless it was relevant to my situation. My family was very accepting of my constant need to emotionally off-load and their kindness helped me meander through my grief.

Kieran returned a few hours later and I felt reassured he needed to be with me again. But instead of wanting to stay, he dropped another clanger.

'I'm going to take the au pair, Marie, hill-walking.'

'What did you say?' I thought I'd misheard.

'I'm taking Jake and Marie to Ballycurragan for a walk. Jake needs it: I haven't walked him properly since we got him back from the kennels. Marie is bored and I think I should show her some of Killaloe.'

I was lost for words. He had only just returned from anti-fouling the boat and now he was bringing our au pair out. How could he bring Marie to the forest walk in Ballycurragan where on Saturdays, I had walked Jake as a pup? How could he be so insensitive? Ballycurragan, a Coilte forest trail with stunning views over Lough Derg, was my forest, my walk.

In that minute I knew I'd lost him. I knew he wanted out. It was all too difficult for him to cope with. He'd stuck by me as best he could, but now he had to go. The fear in my eyes was a clear indicator to Mum what I was thinking. She knew me and knew what was going on.

So when he left, she said, 'Kim, he needs a break. It's been very difficult for him and he needs to get out of the house for a while. That's why I'm here, love. I'm here to help the two of you and take some pressure off your relationship.'

'I've lost him, Mum. He wants to share something that's special to me with another person. I don't care if she's male or female, he should want to be here with me.'

'Now listen here. He loves you very much, cut him a little slack. There's nothing to it.'

'That's not what I mean. I know there's not.'

I went upstairs. The sadness wouldn't lift from me and I howled, cursing expletives at God.

'You bastard! You selfish bastard! Why did you do this? What the hell did I do to deserve this? What the hell does anybody do to deserve this? You do this to people all the time. I FUCKIN' HATE YOU!'

These words hadn't been part of my everyday vocabulary up to this point, but I was angry; I was furious. He'd abandoned me. Day after day words like these flowed from me. There was power in the cursing and the rage was helping me deal with my hurt. If God wasn't to blame, who was? It was easier to put the blame on him than on anybody else. I knew the words were atrocious to use, but I felt I'd be forgiven under the circumstances. Wasn't he supposed to be a forgiving God?

I also shouted at my deceased aunt, Mary Maguire, and pleaded with her to help me. I had loved her more than any of my other aunts. She had really cared about my siblings and me and she had always spent Christmas with us. She'd arrive on Christmas Eve and we would go through her bags, ensuring she had a present for each of us. She always had. But where was my loving aunt now?

After weeks of seeking her support from the heavens, I realised she wasn't going to help me. I was still finding it hard to manage and was mad with her for not helping me. There was nobody left to ask. I was alone trying to cope with both my disability and my failing relationship with my husband.

An overdose could put an end to this pain.

But pictures of women destitute in places like Rwanda came into my mind. I knew there were others going through worse things than me – mothers watching their children being mutilated, murdered, raped and tortured. Had I a right to be so selfish? These visions of war and displacement temporarily silenced my self-pity and defused my anger.

I looked over at a photograph of Kieran and I laughing in the sun on a holiday a few years ago. I closed my eyes and urged myself to think of happier times out on the ocean waves, sailing.

Sailing in Croatia

2007

OUR passion and indulgences were our holidays. We chartered sailing boats from Dubrovnik and Split in Croatia, and Puerto Pollensa in Majorca. The sailing boats we hired were sparkling white, beautifully designed with shiny wooden-fixtures and were large enough to sleep six adults, although with my number of clothes and need for space, two people on board was perfect. Each boat had a small galley kitchen, two double berths, a saloon and a tiny wet room with a toilet and a shower. The temperatures down below in the cabin were always high and in the muggy heat we slept separately, Kieran in the spacious aft-cabin and me in the bow. We'd leave the hatches open to air the boat and to encourage a little breeze to blow through.

Kieran was a well-experienced sailor. We were self-sufficient out on the water and as the wind would catch the mainsail and the jib, we were catapulted from our working-home lives into paradise for two weeks. It was escapism and they were holidays we never took for granted. We were in an enviable position to be able to afford the cost of the charter and experience sailing in the turquoise waters of the Mediterranean and Adriatic Seas.

'Kieran will you tell me what to do? I haven't a clue,' I asked him as we set off from Dubrovnik on the first sailing holiday.

I was nervous and wasn't too sure if I wanted to stay on a boat for two weeks.

'Could we not have stayed in a hotel?' I asked him.

'No, not this time. Relax, you'll love it. You've nothing to do but sun-bathe. Enjoy yourself.'

'Mmm, I don't know about that.'

But it didn't take long to get into the swing of things. Kieran was the skipper and I jokingly called myself 'Deck-boy.' He watched the wind, reefed the sails and plotted the course. I, on the other hand, took off my bikini, lathered myself in sun-cream and sizzled.

'Hey! The sail is shading me. Can you change the boat's position so the sun isn't behind the sail?'

'Again? I've just put in a tack. At this rate we'll never get to Korcula Island.'

It didn't matter to me if I was adding a half hour to our journey. It wasn't about the destination; we were free and time was no longer a noose around our necks. Sometimes when Kieran refused to listen to my vain suntan needs, I'd have to lift my cushion-bed, towel and David Baldacci thriller to the other side of the boat in search of uninterrupted sun.

However, when we were approaching the shore line I abdicated my bossy stance. Our relationship now reverted to that of my parents' when they were farming. The man was the boss and the woman the crew. This was Kieran's area of expertise and for many reasons including safety, I relinquished my position.

My one and only job was to learn how to use the electric windlass to release the anchor chain when we were mooring the boat. I had asked Kieran if we could practice the procedure out on the water to make sure I could do it correctly when we would have to reverse the boat into the pier and tie up. He told me not to be ridiculous.

'All you've to do is press the button either up or down. It's brainless!'

Korcula was in the distance and there was a buzz both on the water and ashore. Many boats were lined up against the quayside. There were boats of every length and make. Huge motor-cruisers over 100-feet-long blended with other private luxury-yachts and catamarans worth over a million euros.

Professional crews dressed in navy uniforms worked hard on yachts. They were looking after some of the rich who were on their holidays. The white decks sparkled as the crew hosed them down. Nothing was rationed – their water-tanks never ran out mid-shower (as ours had that morning). Some had swimming pools either on the bow or aft decks. Beautifully upholstered leatherette-seats surrounding the pools and decks were more luxurious than any couches displayed in the monstrous estate-houses in *Hello!* magazine.

It was captivating looking at the enormous beasts which took up more quayside than any other boats and dwarfed the local fishing boats, the tourist day-trip boats and the smaller chartered boats. I was in awe but not envious. I was very happy walking our decks, putting fenders over the sides of the boat and tying up the ropes.

Kieran reversed the boat into the quayside in Korcula.

'Press the anchor-button down!' he shouted at me as he threw two ropes to a teenager who had decided to help us on the shore. The boy held the two lines and pulled the boat back waiting for the anchor to dig into the seabed at the front of the bow. I did what I was told and could hear the motor of the chain unfurling from the cleat. The boat continued to reverse. Two Croats were pointing up to me. I was doing everything right. I was pressing the down-button, the chain was working and I assumed they were pointing at something Kieran had failed to do. But the boat was bumping off the harbour wall and the boys were trying to prevent damage to the Bavaria 32 – worth over €40,000. Kieran walked up the deck to the bow where I was bent down holding the electric-control. He looked in horror and pointed to the anchor-well beside my foot.

'You never threw in the anchor!' He roared, trying hard to be patient.

'But the chain was going around the cleat.'

'Yeah, but going nowhere.'

I said nothing and stayed sitting on the deck defeated. It was going to be a long two weeks. Kieran went back to the cockpit put the boat into gear and drove forward again.

The boy who was holding onto the ropes let them go. The boat moved forward.

'This time throw in the anchor before you press any buttons!' He suggested smartly.

I was sulking because I had asked him to rehearse this manoeuvre only half-an-hour before. Now, I was being made a fool of in front of tourists and locals. He had never said anything about throwing the anchor into the water before I released the chain with the button. I was annoyed and I knew he was too.

When the boat was safely tied up, I walked back to the cockpit and he apologised for shouting at me.

'But you never explained it properly.'

'OK I didn't. But I didn't realise you needed to be told.'

He was patient because he was afraid I would abandon ship, and as this had always been his dream for the two of us to sail in the Adriatic Sea, he couldn't take the risk of me disappearing to a hotel and he left alone on the boat. So instead, he gave me a hug and I started to melt. I couldn't be mad with someone I loved so much.

When we regained some of our composure, Kieran fixed the gangway plank from the boat to the shore. Coyly joining the spectators, we now sat in the same cafés as they did, and smirked at Germans, Italians and Austrians making similar mistakes. It was a relief to see I was not the only novice completing this exercise – although Kieran did point out that none of their errors were due to pure stupidity like mine. I ignored his comment and I too became one of the smugly-sniggering boat experts.

Being on the water all day and with the wind on our faces was making us drowsy, so we napped. I lay on the cushions in my cabin looking at the blue sky through my open-hatch window. The hum of different languages being spoken by sailors, who were moored beside us, was fading from my ears because another reverberation above me was more rhythmic and sleep-inducing. There is a comforting sound of halyards beating against the mast that just makes you want to lie still and be engulfed by the jingle.

An hour later, I woke with a start upon hearing footsteps on the stairs. The sound motivated me to stop reminiscing and get out of the bed. Kieran had returned from his walk with the au pair and dog. He opened the bedroom door and he pretended to get something out of the wardrobe. I knew he was sussing out the situation – were we talking or not?

Using some inner strength, I said, 'Give me one year before you leave, just a year until I'm on my feet again. Then you can go.'

He turned to me, his cheeks red with fury and roared into my face, 'How could you? How could you say that to me? I've kept you alive. I've fought tooth and nail for you and you'd think I'd leave you now? You've absolutely no idea what I've been through, thinking I was losing you. You haven't a clue, and now you've the audacity to say I'm leaving.

'I collapsed onto the floor when you were being brought into theatre. I was powerless. I thought you were dead. I thought my life was over. How could you? I'm going nowhere. Maybe you'd prefer if I did?'

He looked at me straight in the eye and my face started to burn. He was turning the tables on me and I didn't know how to progress this confrontation any further.

He continued, 'What's going on? It's always about you. You, You, You! I need some space every so often. I need to go to the boat. I need to go for walks.'

'But that's my walk and you brought someone else with you. I wanted to go. I don't want this disability in our lives.'

'You had the stroke, not me! It didn't happen to me, it happened to you! I need my own life at times.'

Up until this moment I had thought the stroke happened to both of us. It did in many ways, but physically Kieran was unaffected. His limbs were all intact. He wasn't hemiplegic. It was inevitable that at some stage on this journey our lives needed to unglue from one another. He was right, the stroke had happened to me, but the reality of this was a huge blow and it was starting to dawn on me, I'd need to stop being so dependent on him and start being more active in my recovery.

He stomped towards the bedroom door, slammed it shut and I could hear the thumping of his feet on the stairs, and the front door banging shut. I was put in my place and even though I was embarrassed, I was happy I hadn't lost him.

Mum came upstairs to me and put her arms around my shoulders.

'Would the two of you like to go out for a drink tonight?'

'Mum, I'm just exhausted. Dylan wakes at least three times a night and Kieran gets up to feed him and comfort him. I lie in bed, stuck on my back and not able to help. Even if I get up, put my shoes and orthotic on, I still can't lift Dylan to feed or change him. Last night Kieran was too tired to get up for the fourth time and I lay crying because I wanted to cuddle and mind my little baby. What mother lies in bed listening to their upset child and finds herself incapacitated to comfort him?'

'I know love, but I'm here now and I'll take Dylan tonight to let the two of you sleep, but go out for a drink first.'

My new regime

THIS was my first public appearance in my village and I was apprehensive. Kieran pulled up outside the pub. I managed to get out of the car but the apprehension in my body caused my muscles to tighten and my leg went into spasm.

'Relax Kim, you'll be fine. Put your leg on the ground. It'll be grand. Are you ready to go in?' Kieran asked.

There weren't many punters in the pub at this early time of the evening and I followed Kieran to a quiet section of the pub where we used always sit before. I sat down. We'd been gone from our 'local' a long time. I lifted my head. Nothing had changed. Logs smouldered in the fire to the left of me and the smell of smoke tickled my nose. Wobbly chairs with different leg-lengths hadn't been replaced by modern health-and-safety-conforming chairs. The atmosphere was the same, still full of character. The pub hadn't been touched by the Celtic Tiger and it looked like it wasn't going to be modernised in austere times either. A relief for the regulars, I'm sure.

'What would you like to drink, Kim and Kieran?' the pub owner asked us, tentatively approaching our table.

'A pint and a juice, please.'

By the time the drinks were served, two friends of ours had joined us. Their jovial conversation was helping me relax. Some acquaintances had come in and were unobtrusively looking our way. No one was blatantly staring: I'd be yesterday's news by tomorrow. It was all going very well. Our community knew what had happened and were rallying around.

After a while Kieran looked me at in the eye and I said, 'People really care, don't they? I can't believe the kindness everywhere. It's very touching.'

'Quite amazing, isn't it? You're doing great, Kim. Do you want another drink?'

'Sure why not?'

Our group increased to six and at times I was able to engage fully in the conversation; other times I withdrew into myself. I was remembering the going-away party we'd had in the very same pub when drinks were flowing and the excitement was contagious.

'I think I'd like to get home Kieran,' I said, putting down my empty glass of orange juice. I wanted to use the toilet but it was at the far end of the pub. Exposing my disability any further by asking people to move out of my way was a step too far on this outing of mine.

We got up to leave and like Moses parting the waters, a group chatting near the doorway subtly stood back making a passage way for us to get to the door. No one turned to stare, no fuss, just a slight shuffle of feet and a small manoeuvre of a bar-stool or two.

The collective support I felt was somewhat overwhelming. Most people living in our village either knew us well or knew us to see and wanted to offer encouragement in any way they could. The kind unspoken words, the empathetic looks and the care which was shown that night and for many years to come were an endorsement we were living in the best place in Ireland.

A new week began and I started to get involved in my rehabilitation. I'd once said to Kostas that I'd have to return to Cyprus to avail of the services which were readily available there. But I didn't have to. The HSE provided all I needed. I'd been looked after in the NRH and now on my return home my case-manger allocated me some hours with a rehabilitation assistant, a psychologist and a personal assistant. I couldn't have asked for more. I had also arranged three private physiotherapy sessions a week, two in a clinic and another in a hydrotherapy pool in Limerick. All in all, including my au pair, I was trying to organise a group of six people, sometimes even more when friends and family came to help.

The care was invaluable and without it my recovery would not have advanced as far as it was going to, and yet my life was not my own. I was giving little bits of me to others in my endeavour to rehabilitate as best as I could. Juggling my therapies and my 'staff' took a lot of organising and concentration. Being a mother to my son was my first prerogative. I needed to get better as soon as possible but Dylan needed me now. I was in turmoil. How could I manage my time? Therapies were consuming and necessary but I wanted to be with my only child.

'I love Dylan so much but I've to get stronger on my feet. How can I handle both, without compromising the other?' I asked my rehabilitation assistant, Emma, before we started my exercise programme for the morning.

Emma often listened to my pleas of help where my disability and Dylan were concerned, and invariably put my mind to rest for a little while.

'You're strong, Kim, you'll be able to do both. Many women have to juggle working full-time and they might only get to be with their children for an hour or so before the child has to go to bed. Your rehabilitation is a full-time job: you finish it by 3 or 4 p.m. If you were back teaching your day would be mapped out in a similar fashion. Don't be too hard on yourself.'

'You have a point. I suppose my rehab is like a job. I want to succeed, I want to get better.'

I looked into her kind face.

'I'm a mother too,' she said, 'and I can see where you're coming from, but it will all work out in the end. Please believe me, things always do.'

'I'm lost, I'm alone. I'm a different person on the outside and that's causing inner conflict. Look how your lipstick coordinates with your clothes and how your scarf picks out the colours in your top. That used to be me. I used to plan my wardrobe the night before I went to work. My brown boots would be neatly placed beside my matching leather bag, my skirts would hang beside freshly ironed tops and my nail

269

varnish was immaculate. Nothing was haphazard, nothing was left to chance.'

'You're going to get that back again. You will care about your looks – you just need to work through some things first,' Emma said.

I had to believe this woman, a woman the same age as me, a woman who cared about her appearance. A wise woman.

Our conversation finished and it was time for work.

'Come on, let's go into the sitting-room and get started,' she said.

My rehabilitation assistant rolled out my floormat and I lay down on the mat and turned my head to the side. The sand-coloured carpet in the 'good-room' had a peculiar smell which I hadn't noticed before. It was a mixture of musk and well-worn wool threads and each time I rolled backwards into a lying position on the floor, I could get the subtle whiff from the fibres. I hoped Emma was unable to smell the unpleasant musky carpet too, when she was kneeling beside me.

We spent an hour and a half doing floor exercises and it was then time for hand stretches at the kitchen table. As we ventured into the kitchen, I heard the unmistakable crying of Dylan who was in my au pair's arms. His cheeks were red under his tears as he had been up a lot during the night and I knew he was off-form.

I approached him and stroked his tubby little hand but he pulled away and snuggled into Marie. I put my arm out for her to let me hug him but he didn't want to come to me. I spoke to him softly trying to comfort him, but he was upset. Marie and the rehabilitation assistant looked at me. I felt inadequate in front of the two females in my home and I didn't know what to do next.

'Maybe take him outside and see if the fresh air helps soothe him,' I said to her.

She brought Dylan out onto the deck and bounced him up and down. I was relieved to hear him giggle and knew he'd settle down soon – I could continue my work and I was no longer exposed as an inept mother who couldn't console her baby.

'What am I going to do? I can't comfort him!' I said to Kieran when he came home from work later. 'I'm afraid I'm losing Dylan's trust. I wasn't there for him in the first six months of his life and perhaps he doesn't trust me to stay with him now.'

'He's only seven months old. He needs food and nappy changes but most of all he needs love. You love him and he knows that. He might not go to you at the moment when he's upset because he wants to be lifted; but you're his mother and that will never change. A mother's love is eternal and consistent. People will come in and out of his life but you're the one person he will always rely on. Believe me.'

'But episodes like this have happened before. It seems as though he prefers you, or Mum or the au pair. I love him beyond anything I've ever known and I'll never give up on that love.'

'I'm sure you're not the first parent to ever have feelings of inadequacy. But your feelings of incompetence are completely unfounded. You're coming to terms with a disability and are

271

trying to find ways of compensating for the new body you have. You're not failing. You're learning new ways to care for Dylan – methods none of us have had to learn. I feel inadequate too when I'm unable to comfort him and you can. He recognises your voice when you sing to him, he senses your calm energy. Never say you're an inadequate mother. Your mothering skills are mind-blowing at times. You're teaching me how to be a patient and loving parent.'

'That's lovely to say but my confidence is so low I don't know if I can believe you.'

'Somewhere deep down you do believe me. I bet Thomas will agree. Why don't you explain this to him?'

Give Dylan back

I KNEW I'd need to discuss this with Thomas, the psychologist, who was due to come to the house any minute. I'd so many things to deliberate over with him and when we did get to talk, I started despairingly, 'Hard work has always paid off before, so why won't it now? I've worked hard for my Leaving Cert, passed exams in college and gave birth to a baby – against all the odds. I'll succeed in this endeavour too. In two years' time, I'll be perfect again.'

'What does it feel like saying this?'

'Em...'

But by then I had already altered my position.

'I'm not sure if I believe it to be honest. I'm terrified I won't succeed.'

I was staring out the panoramic window in the sitting room. The river was glistening in the low evening sun and I could see a boat pulling into a marina on the other side of the river. I looked at Thomas's face searching for an answer but he was giving nothing away.

'Have you worked with other people like me?'

What I really wanted to know was if he had a magic cure which he'd successfully used on others to make them better.

'What do you mean?'

'Women who've had post-partum stroke, who've lost half of their bodies at the most important time of their lives. Women like me who wanted to be there for their new-borns but were robbed of that experience.'

I started to wail as I acknowledged my loss.

'He's beautiful. Look behind me into the kitchen. Marie's out there, strutting around with him in her arms. It should be me. I've wanted to do that since I was a little girl; cuddle and kiss babies.'

'What's it like for you seeing him in her arms?'

'It's awful. He cries and someone lifts him up to comfort him. It's not just her, people are trying to help but they keep taking him from me, never thinking to ask me if they can or if I'd like him back.'

'Go on.'

'It's like I'm invisible, useless, not worthy of my own child. For example, the other day a friend chastised Dylan in front of me. I was sitting next to her as she was dressing Dylan for me. She gave out to him for being uncooperative. I was there! Imagine that, I was there! She ignored my right. She ignored the mother-child relationship. If I had been able-bodied I would have been dressing my son myself. Would she have given out to him in front of me then? No of course not. How dare she! He's mine. I'll do any chastising if ever needed.'

'How do you think you could change your role in something like that if it ever happens again?'

I thought for a few minutes.

'I suppose if I was brave enough I'd say; "when I'm with you, you're my hands, just my hands. I'm Dylan's mother and I'll do the comforting or whatever else needs to be done. However, if I'm not around your relationship changes. You're in charge of him and you can use your discretion as to what he might need."

'But the difference between the two roles is very subtle. How in God's name do I get that across to a friend or family member without insulting them? They've offered me help and then I hurt them by asking them to back off, to stop cuddling or doing something that's innately instinctive to a human being. They might never help me again.'

'Whose relationship is more important, yours and Dylan's or yours and your friends?'

'Mine and my child's of course but when I asked a friend to help me bath Dylan the other night, as she was taking him out of the bath, Dylan started to cry. Her automatic response was to put him over her shoulder to comfort him. I was an observer.'

'Why didn't you ask for him?'

Running the scenario over in my mind, I had to be honest with Thomas about my shame and concerns.

'I thought Dylan wouldn't want to come to me and he'd get more upset if she placed him on my knee. She might end up taking him from me anyway and I'd be even more hurt and exposed.'

'So you think he wouldn't go to you. Tell me more.'

The weekly sessions continued in this manner. I'd start the hour's session bereft and finish it feeling a little more optimistic. I knew what was needed going forward – I needed to get back control over my life. I had to remember to monitor what was going on in the house and what was happening to Dylan. The power was actually within my grasp if I had enough courage to grab it.

My confidence was beginning to grow every month and one day I asked Kieran if he'd accompany me to my work-place and meet my colleagues I hadn't met yet since our return from Cyprus.

'That sounds like a good plan. I'll collect you after physiotherapy today.'

'What'll I wear? I've no idea what to wear. Maybe I'll find a top I used to wear before my stroke,' I said, thinking about my wardrobe full of beautiful outfits I'd once purchased from stores all over Ireland. Clothes had been my hobby, my passion.

I must be beginning to put effort into my appearance if I'm wondering what to wear.

The staffroom in my school hadn't changed a bit. The shelves were still full of books no one ever read and the noticeboard showed a timetable for the teachers' yard duty. Weekly yard duty was my least favourite half hour of the week. I'd try to break up fights between children, whilst shivering in my fleece-lined coat, covered in sticky paw-marks from gorgeous little children hitting my thigh trying to catch my attention: 'Teacher, teacher, I need go toilet!'

It felt strange visiting such a familiar place with Kieran, Dylan and the 'new-disabled me'. I had probably eaten over 1,000 lunches in this room but now it was a foreign land full of well-meaning smiles and awkwardness. I felt for my self-conscious colleagues – what do you say to a co-worker who has suffered a stroke, who had always been 'glam Kim,' but was now skin-and-bone Kim?

Dylan was a welcome distraction and Kieran was talking for the three of us. I lifted my sullen head and made eye-contact with my good friend Jo (one of the people I'd often phoned from my hospital bed, disorientated and desperate for something I didn't understand I needed). She smiled with encouragement which helped me to soften and accept the genuine kindness and support which was on offer.

'I was in France on holidays when I got the text to say you'd a baby boy,' a colleague said. 'I was overjoyed for you both and bought a baby present straight away. Then a week later I looked at my phone to see five missed calls. I knew something bad must have happened to someone. When I heard you'd had a brain haemorrhage. I just couldn't believe it!'

It hadn't occurred to me that news of my illness had travelled so fast and so far in a very short time, and it was nice people cared so much. I heard many similar stories from my co-workers, and by the time we'd each had three cups of tea, eaten a box of Afternoon Tea biscuits, it was time to leave.

My life was becoming bearable once more. The only way was up.

Another stroke?

SOPHIE rocked a little when John and Kieran heaved me up onto her deck and into the cockpit. John, our friend from Cyprus, had come for dinner. It was 6.00 p.m. and there was still warmth in the June sun. We were right to take this opportunity to go for a sail with our friend.

John and Kieran got aboard too and I sat in the cockpit listening to Kieran telling John to take in the fenders. Anytime we had gone for an evening sail with friends after work, I had automatically slipped into my crew-role but now I was relinquishing all control of any sailing knowledge I'd accumulated over the years, and was handing it over to John who had never sailed before.

The calm water flickered on either side of the boat. After a while Kieran asked John to steer the boat so he could go down to the galley to put a ready-made lasagne in the oven. John and I were left alone.

'How are you doing now Kim?' he asked me.

'I'm good thanks, John. It's not even a year yet. I'm getting through each day as best as I can. There have been some days I haven't even cried – a huge improvement I think. Overall I'm very good.'

'You look great!'

'Not as good as I did before!' I smirked, tongue-in-cheek.

I was relaxed in John's company. When Kieran and I had first arrived in Cyprus, we had stayed in his house for a few days. We'd spent many evenings with his wife, Ann, and their kids in Andy's Bar and at barbeques. I'd forgotten the good banter John and I had back then and his witty sense of humour which could make a whole pub laugh. A week before John and Ann, left the island to return home, they'd visited me briefly in hospital to say goodbye. It was only ten days after my brain surgery and I could clearly make out the tremor in their voices when they stood close to the bed to hug me.

John and I hadn't seen each other since and there was much to catch up on. Ann had recently had a baby and John proudly showed me a photo of their new arrival, a beautiful baby boy.

Every time I saw a photo of a new-born, the first thoughts which came into my head were always directed towards the infant.

You're lucky your Mummy will get to hold, lift and stroke you.

I chastised myself. It was about time I put my jealousy aside. I was thrilled for them and I quickly cast away my envy.

'He looks gorgeous! Congratulations to the two of you.'

'Thanks, he's a great kid and we spoil him rotten. Kim, it's so nice seeing you look so healthy. The two of you seem to be doing extraordinarily well.'

'Yeah, I think we're getting there,' Kieran said, passing plates and cutlery up to John on the deck.

I started to smile.

'Do you remember one of the early days when we were on the beach in Pyla?'

John nodded.

'I was sunbathing oblivious to any of our group on the beach.'

'I think I know where this is going,' John replied, the heat rising in his cheeks.

'I was reading my book in peace and you decided to come over to be sociable.'

'Beaches aren't my thing. I needed to get up and find someone to chat to.'

Kieran started to laugh as he remembered the incident clearly. 'You caught my chick sunbathing topless!'

'And,' I continued, 'when I put down my book, which was blocking your view, you were so startled you said, "Oh, boobies!" and pointed at me.'

John blushed again and started to laugh.

'What's worse, I had to go into work an hour later and face Kieran.'

Kieran added, 'Kim had already phoned me to tell me what happened and when I asked you had you a nice time on the beach, you went as red as a tomato.'

'Well, in fairness, it's not every day you see your sergeant's wife's tits! I didn't know where to look.'

Events which happened in Cyprus kept us laughing throughout the dinner, and when we said goodbye to him later that night, I'd a strong inner glow of happiness.

Kieran and I returned to the house and sat in the sitting room for a while. We reminisced about good times and it felt good.

'I'm going to bed now, Kieran,' I said, when it started to get dark.

I got undressed and sat up in the bed to read while Kieran was checking on Dylan.

Suddenly a strange pulsing sensation started to whirl inside my foot. It was something I'd never experienced before and it was frightening.

'Kieran, Kieran!' I screamed. 'Something really strange is happening.'

He hadn't heard me, so I roared once more, 'Kieran, come here!'

He knew from the tone of my voice something was wrong and ran into our bedroom.

'What's the matter? What is it?'

'I can't feel my leg or my arm. Help me Kieran! Help me!'

'Do you want me to phone an ambulance?'

I nodded, thinking I would change my mind in a second or two and tell him not to, but as I watched him dial 999 on the phone beside the bed, I didn't tell him to hang up. Things were becoming serious. The rhythmic swirling movement which had started in my left foot, was travelling the whole way up my leg, past my waist, through my arm, up my neck and finally into my head. The heat I felt inside my body was intense. I lost consciousness.

Later Kieran told me that he shouted at Marie to wake up and mind Dylan. She was listening to music and hadn't heard. He yelled really loud, waking Dylan from his light slumber and causing him to get upset. My husband couldn't leave my side – the thoughts of my previous stroke consumed his every thought.

'The ambulance will be here soon. Don't die Kim. Hold on in there, we need you. Stay alive for us: WAKE UP!'

He dialled 999 again.

'Where's the ambulance? My wife's having a stroke. Hurry up for God's sake.'

He watched as my body contorted and shook uncontrollably. All of a sudden he noticed a frothing at my mouth; offering him a little hope I might be having a seizure and not a stroke. But it was terrifying and Dylan's crying was upsetting too – as though he sensed something terrible was happening.

I started to come to, but my eyelids felt heavy and I struggled to keep my eyes open. I was sitting on a gurney and was being lifted down our stairs. A female paramedic was facing me, directing her male colleague navigate the turn in the staircase. The extra banister on the wall obstructed the already narrow staircase. They tugged and twisted the gurney.

I bet the carpet is getting dirty from their boots. Oh no the wall! They've just scraped the paintwork.

During my lengthy summer holidays from teaching, I'd often painted the interior of our house. I'd listened to Gerry Ryan on the radio, happily immersed in my own world. Gerry Ryan was now gone and I hadn't the same jurisdiction over my body to do the work I wanted to.

I guess the scrapes on the walls are here to stay. My standards have to drop. Does it really matter anymore?

The siren screeched as the ambulance manoeuvred in and out of traffic. I felt queasy and wasn't quite sure what was going on.

'Do think you're going to be sick?' the female paramedic asked, tucking a blanket around my feet.

'No, I don't think so. I don't know what happened. I don't know where I am and I don't know where my husband is.'

'It's OK, don't worry. Your husband is following us to The Mid-West Hospital where a doctor will take a look at you.'

A&E was the first sign I saw when the ambulance stopped outside the hospital in Limerick. Disbelief was written across my face.

Here we go again; another hospital; another illness. When would it all stop?

'Where's my wife Kim? She was brought in here by ambulance.'

'She's in Cubicle 4,' a nurse replied.

Kieran pulled back the curtain and I was a relieved to see his face. He came over to the side of my bed, kissed me, and held my hand.

'What happened, Kieran?'

'I think you might have had a seizure, Kim. That's what it looked like to me, but we're waiting for the neurologist to take a look at you. Do you remember Rasmus's seizure in Cyprus in the physiotherapy clinic? It looked a bit like that.'

'I'm sorry, Kieran.'

'There's no need to be. It's not your fault. Is there no end to what we have to go through?' Kieran said, subdued and emotionally drained in the knowledge he'd have to take on even more responsibility for my well-being.

Kieran's head was bent down and he was still holding my hand. It felt as though we were back to square one again: me in hospital and him keeping the show on the road. He probably had the more difficult job of the two of us, feeling helpless, having to put on a brave face and organising both Dylan and me. Once more he'd have to phone work to let them know he couldn't go in.

My heart went out to him. I had no idea what my husband was going through at that moment. I did know how terrifying it was for him when I'd lost consciousness eleven months previously in Cyprus, but at that time Kieran hadn't realised just how serious the situation was. He had thought it was food poisoning and non-life threatening. Now, he was acutely aware what a stroke looked like, and that in itself must have made the night's seizure even more frightening for him.

'I phoned your Mum to ask her to come down and help for a few days. Marie needs the weekend off and I need help with Dylan and you.'

I felt awful having to look to my family for more help. They had been a fantastic support to us for so long and with their assistance we had been doing very well over the months. I really wanted to be able to live without outside help, but not being in control of my own health, I'd no choice but to ask for more support.

'We have to cancel the christening,' I said drowsily. 'It's in a few days' time. I don't know if I'll be strong enough for it.'

'We'll see, you'll be fine by then.'

Dylan's christening

THE church in Ballina looks over the azure water of the Shannon which flows slowly towards the power-station in Ardnacrusha in County Clare. I stood at the church door and took in the vista. It was unusually humid, there wasn't a cloud in the sky and it was near perfect. My son was being christened and I was his proud mother who had given birth to him a year before. My motherly instincts were to the fore and I was beginning to feel like the 'proper' mother I was constantly striving to be.

We went inside and the priest invited Kieran and me to stand at the water-font on the altar. The font was made of granite. My deceased grandfather had owned a stone-quarry in County Wicklow, producing much of the granite for the buildings in Dublin city centre. Whilst I had never met my father's father, I felt his presence and whispered to him to give me the strength to get through the day.

Dylan started to cry as the Holy Water was generously poured on his forehead. He looked up at his parents beseechingly. I leant into Kieran's strong arm which held our precious bundle and I stroked the warm cheeks of our not-too-happy son.

'Hush little baby. It's OK, it's all finished now.'

When Dylan was baptised and welcomed as a new member of the Catholic Church, we drove towards the restaurant for his christening lunch.

The sun filtered through the Velux-windows in the restaurant. Beams and rafters of solid pine were absorbing the sun's rays and little dust particles danced in the sun's glow. Generously varnished wooden floors and tables reflected the light which was also beaming through the floor-to-ceiling windows. Patrons were enjoying their lunches and children were running in and out of the restaurant to the garden to climb a large conifer tree, roll on the grass and enjoy the weather.

The green of the grass in the garden contrasted the blue of the Shannon which was sluggishly flowing behind the garden. Ripples on the water were twinkling like diamonds and were only disrupted by the odd hired-cruiser carrying families from Killaloe up the spine of the country to Athlone. It was the start of the busy holiday season.

An eager waitress approached us with her notebook. We ordered and as I put the menu aside I looked around the table. This was a special group of people and whilst I was OK with our decision not to invite all of our family members to the christening, there was a sense of loss they weren't with us. I felt sad I hadn't had the strength to share this day with a larger number of people.

The arrival of our food interrupted my thoughts.

'Are you getting another au pair?' Kieran's brother, Fergal, asked lifting a cup of vegetable soup to his lips.

'Yes, we'll have to when Marie leaves next month,' I replied, trying to cut a slice of chicken I'd yet to touch on my plate. 'We've no choice really, now that I'm not driving. I need someone to drive me to physiotherapy and to the crèche. I still need someone to lift Dylan, change his nappies, bath him and put him to bed. I wish we didn't have to, but it's just the way things are.'

I gave up trying to cut my meat and asked Fergal to help me.

'You've been lucky with Marie. She's been great, hasn't she?' Dylan's godmother, Carla added.

'Yes she has. She loves Dylan to bits and has been no trouble. I didn't know what to make of her at the start and it was hard when she was able to mind Dylan in a way I wasn't. But in fairness we couldn't have asked for better. She's not a bit needy and doesn't really do emotion which is helpful as there's enough upset going on in the house without her feelings getting in the way. However, when the chips are down, she's able to pull out all the stops. To be honest, we're dreading her leaving.'

The heat was getting to everyone, shirt-collars were open, jackets were hanging on chairs and trips in and out to the garden were becoming increasingly frequent.

'Photo time. Everyone outside!' Kieran demanded when the desserts were finished.

Lining up as requested, we smiled into the camera lens and he clicked one photo after the next. The day's events were pictorially documented.

'I think we'd better get Dylan home for his nap,' I said. Tiredness was creeping in. It had been a long day.

We said our goodbyes and I was grateful when Kieran, Dylan I returned to our home on our own.

My bed looked inviting and I got into it with Dylan. I was happy by the success of the day's events. I had got through the day and hadn't cried in front of anyone.

A mother at last

2011

THE following year I was allowed to drive again, and we didn't need to have an au pair. Without the extra person in our home, I was able to take sole ownership of my son. I had to learn various tasks which she would have done and I was nervous Dylan wouldn't respond to me or my authority. Motherhood was something I couldn't fail at no matter how difficult it was going to be and no matter what lay ahead. He was my son and I would have done anything for him.

'Come on Dylan let's go for a walk,' I said to my two-year-old when we were playing with a little train-set. 'Stand up on the couch there and I'll help you into the buggy.'

I had never brought him for a walk in a pushchair on my own. Things were different and my main aim was for him to trust I could take care of him. I needed to make him feel safe and not sense my apprehension.

He climbed onto the couch and I coaxed him to get his legs into the buggy. I placed my arm under his bottom helping him sit down. One of his legs got caught in the safety-bar of the buggy and he toppled onto the floor.

'Oops, there's a good boy.'

Don't cry.

'My leg hurted.'

'You're such a brave boy, let's try again. Up you go.'

We had many failed attempts, when he either refused to get back onto the couch or go near the buggy. I was at his mercy – we could only do something if he was in agreement because lifting him into the pram or into the car wasn't a possibility for me.

He started to cry and threw himself onto the floor in frustration. I felt like doing the same so I abandoned the walk. I'd try again tomorrow.

'Come on let's take out your Peppa Pig jigsaw.'

He came over to me and he helped me take the lid off the box.

'Good boy, where does this piece go?'

He put the piece of the jigsaw on my head and I pretended I couldn't see it. We laughed hysterically.

The game went on for quite a while.

The afternoon passed with little incident until I realised he'd been in the same nappy since I'd collected him from the crèche four hours prior.

'Have you a wet nappy?'

He nodded.

'Up here,' I said pointing to the couch in the playroom. 'No wait, I've to put the changing-mat underneath you.'

'No want to.'

He wouldn't come over to me. I asked him again to get up onto the couch so I could look at his nappy. He wouldn't. What could I do?

'Dylan, if you have a wet nappy, your bum will sting. Let me know when you want me to change you.'

He ran into the kitchen and I was left alone in the playroom, defeated. It was a bitter pill to swallow – managing on my own was hard. The pain in my chest wouldn't abate.

What kind of mother would leave their child in a wet nappy?

'Dylan, please come here. Please!'

I sounded desperate now.

'No.'

There was a banging sound in the hall. Kieran was home from work and he waltzed into the room to take over.

'Dadda,' Dylan said, running into Kieran's arms.

Kieran did everything I couldn't do and I was envious. He picked Dylan up and he whizzed him into the air. Dylan gurgled as he was swung round and round. I was a stranger. Their bond was exclusive. Kieran felt Dylan's trousers.

'Oh, you've a wet nappy, let's change you.'

I dissipated into thin air and stepped into the kitchen.

'How did the day go for you?' Kieran asked, carrying Dylan in to me.

I went through the events of the day and explained how I'd failed.

'I've never been as proud of you as I am now. You spent your first afternoon on your own with your son and it went great.'

'But he wouldn't get into the buggy or let me change him.'

'Don't be upset. It's your first day. You've one functioning arm, you're shaky on your feet and you're just starting to be confident. I don't know anyone else with your strength. You're amazing! Come on, why don't the three of us go for a walk? I'll help you place him in the buggy and you can push him.'

'Thanks.'

'Are you OK?' Kieran asked, looking at my sullen face.

Words decanted from of my mouth.

'Kieran, please don't come in and take over, you're undoing all the work I've achieved. I feel you're like Mr Fix-It taking Dylan from me and doing all the things I want to do. It's hard for me to be an observer – silently screaming at you. I want to be the one who lifts him into my arms and plant kisses on his nose. I know it's not your fault and you've every right to do it, but please don't exclude me, I'm his Mum.'

'I thought I was helping and you'd need a break. I'm sorry, I'd no idea you felt I was taking him from you.'

That's the problem, no one does.

The next day was completely different. I modified my modus operandi, so instead of bringing the buggy into the equation, we went for a walk on foot.

'Look at the daisies. Let's pick some daisies,' I said to Dylan as we stopped for the umpteenth time to pick leaves and flowers from hedgerows.

I reiterated the word 'daisies' placing emphases on the initial sound. It was if I was back in my teacher-role as language enhancer, except I wasn't. My role was much more important than that. I was his primary educator – his mother who was teaching him love and who was spending uninterrupted time with her little boy.

'No, no; that's a puddle. Don't!'

I was too late.

He was jumping up and down, splashing his cute little jeans and laughing heartily with excitement.

'Muggy puggle,' he said.

'OK, you're right. I don't mind.' I encouraged, having a complete change of heart. 'Yes it's called a puddle, and you're jumping into a puddle. You're like Peppa Pig!'

By now we were on the avenue of our local hotel. I was proud of his dirty face, hands and trousers. For me, it meant we'd been having fun. We strolled hand in hand into the lobby of the hotel. It felt as though I were a regular mother spending time with her child. No one noticed us. No one knew what an achievement this was. I didn't care. It felt amazing and I was beaming all over.

'You've a wet nappy,' I said to Dylan when we got home. 'Let's change it.'

The changing station on the couch was ready to go. I'd got it ready earlier in the day, the waterproof mat, wipes, and new nappies were spread out in front of me.

Dylan jumped onto the couch. His wet shoes and trousers were somewhat awkward to pull off, but I managed to do it. I rubbed my nose on his belly and opened the fasteners of his babygro. I slid his wet nappy from under him, flung it on the floor and then rolled him on his side.

'Good boy, helping Mummy. You're the best boy. I'm wiping your bum with a wipe now, there's the best boy. No, roll back over so Mummy can put your clean nappy on.'

I tried to slide the fresh nappy under him by easing him from one side to the other and getting him to keep his legs in the air. With some difficulty, I slid the nappy up his back, peeled the seals from the sticky tags at the side, and stuck the tags to the front. The nappy was on. Success!

I couldn't fasten the babygro again but that was irrelevant. He was wearing a nappy. One-handed-me had done it.

'Yippee!' We did it. You've a nice clean nappy. I love you so much. Thank you for helping Mummy. You're the best boy, Dylan, and I'm so proud of you.'

'Dylan good boy.'

'Yes Dylan's a great boy. Well done Dylan! Well done Mummy!'

Later, when I heard Kieran's car in the driveway my heart leaped.

'I'd a fabulous day,' I revealed. 'We'd such a brilliant time together.'

Dylan's nappy had fallen off half an hour before Kieran had come home from work, but I didn't mind. It had been attached to his body longer than it had been on the ground and the tiny pools of urine dotted around the wooden floors were testament to my success and not souvenirs of my failure. The only way was up.

'Mummy?' Dylan said when Kieran went outside to put the nappy in the bin.

'Yes.'

'I love you.' He laughed. 'Gotcha. You not know me say that?'

'Oh no! You caught me out again. Next time I'll get you.'

It was a game we used to play over and over again and it made Dylan and me chortle.

He came over to me and snuggled his head into my lap and I stroked his fair hair.

'You were so excited when I was borned,' he told me.

'Yes pet, it was the most amazing time of my life. Holy God didn't send a baby to us for a long time, so when we knew we were going to have a baby we were very excited. You make us very happy.'

'I maded you better.'

'Yes, when I was sick and I'd look into your big brown eyes, I knew I had to learn to walk. Each time I saw you, you made me better. Thank you for doing that for me.'

Now that my relationship with Dylan was what I'd always wanted, it was time for me to put energy back into my friendships.

Revisiting people and places

GOING out in the evenings for a glass of Pinot Grigio was becoming more frequent. Some husbands might prefer their wives weren't out twice a week with their friends, but Kieran was literally pushing me out the door. He could see how well I was and my gallivanting was having a positive effect on the household.

'Let's go for a Christmas night away,' one of my friends, Gail, suggested one evening in September.

'I'll organise it,' I heard myself saying.

Not only was this going to be a brave adventure for me, I'd also committed to arranging it. I wanted to retract those words.

Oh no! The exposure might be too much. My family are the only ones who have helped me to get dressed. I might get stuck and have to ask for help and I've never had that type of intimate relationship before with my friends.

Perhaps Gail had an insight into my thoughts, or maybe she was just being kind, but when I heard her ask, 'Can I share a room with you when we go away?' I was greatly relieved. She would be discreet and maybe it would be OK for her to witness my vulnerability.

I booked a beautiful hotel in Adare for our night away. The excitement within our small group was contagious. The banter in the car on the way to Adare was full-on and I laughed most of the journey. A little too old for hen nights, we were ready for a more grown-up version of sorts. The same amount of make-up, similar volumes of alcohol and constant laughter are obligatory on both occasions.

I parked my car on the side of the road next to the public park in the village and looked up and down the street. The village looked impressive. I was able to see beauty in the medieval architecture, colourful cottages and in my friends.

There was beauty within me too. My relationship with my (now) three-year-old son was very special. I was a worthy mother who had fought tooth and nail to stay alive for her deserving child. Beautiful inside and out, I no longer retreated from people from my past nor withdrew from my disabled body in the mirror. Time does heal. Yes, it was still my fault I'd had the stroke – I'd definitely done something wrong, but I was able to supress thoughts of shame whenever they came to the fore.

'Let's check-in,' I suggested.

High gothic ceilings and a large Christmas tree dominated the reception hall of the hotel. Christmas lights twinkled all around us adding a sense of magic and wonder to a spectacular ambiance. Persian rugs, chandeliers and antique furniture were part of the décor in this manor house hundreds of years old. Rectangular windows framed the beauty of the outdoor sculptured gardens.

As we stood at the reception desk waiting for our room keys, we caught each other's eyes. We were definitely in the right place: a five-star hotel for seven five-star women. I'd chosen well.

The room key in one hand, and five non-functioning curled fingers in the other, I wondered how I'd manage to get my suitcase to my 'disabled' room. The problem didn't lie in the left fingers or arm; rather the problem was with my weak leg and unsteady body, which could cause me to topple over at any stage.

Wealthy Americans use porters – the Irish can 'manage my luggage myself.' Without even thinking of asking a porter for assistance (how much do you tip him anyway?) I waited for one of my friends to offer help. I needn't have worried; my case was already en train. Johanna had taken it from under my nose and was wheeling both hers and mine. Like the help I got from the contingents in Cyprus, Irish people had things under control before I'd to ask. In Ballina - Killaloe there was always someone to carry my shopping into the car, help me around the house and place Dylan into his car-seat. It was all done in a hair's breadth. No fuss.

Perhaps the survival of the human race rests on the relationships we have with one another. My friends and family were ensuring I'd survive, through their acceptance and care. My physiological needs were being met. I felt safe, I was surrounded by love and my self-esteem was increasing.

Life was worth living.

Our night away was successful. My disability was far from my mind. I was just one of the girls, as I'd always been.

The 'semblance of normality' Kieran had once spoken of was all around us. He was no longer on high alert. He could relax and knew I wouldn't have another stroke, a seizure or an

299

emotional break-down. We were back to real-living, and the good times I spent with friends played a part in rebuilding our relationship.

There was happiness in our home too. I was caring for Dylan each day. My son trusted that I wouldn't leave him and I trusted in my abilities as a mother. We had the relationship I had been looking for and it was exceedingly satisfying.

There was one thing I wanted to do and that was to go back and revisit people and places which had been instrumental in my recovery. The first place I revisited was the National Rehabilitation Hospital.

Going to the NRH as a visitor was poles apart to being an in-patient. I was a very different person.

My hand trembled a little when I drove in through the front gate and I could see building work to the front of the main building.

Were they improving the showering facilities at last?

I hoped so, for my friend's sake. He too had suffered a stroke and I'd come to visit him – to offer him support and to show him things do get better. It felt strange returning. I was now there as someone who had survived an atrocity and had come out the other side.

The same lift brought me down to the ground floor. I stepped back in time. It had only been three-and-a-half years since I'd been here, but nothing had been erased from my memory. The heat of the hospital brought back memories of night-time bed sweats. The corridors were the same, the inner garden was still the focal point and the staff appeared similar. Patients walked or wheeled themselves around the passage-ways. I studied their disabilities and their faces, looking for my mirror-image but no one filled that image. I couldn't see anyone who seemed to be going through the same trauma I had gone through.

Physiotherapists in white polo-shirts and blue trousers streamed by me on their way to the canteen and I no longer felt subservient. I was walking with my head held high and was confidently strolling through my memories. I had survived a stroke and was thriving in the big bad world. I had been rehabilitated.

Look at me!

The faces were friendly and many staff (nurses and orderlies) said hello to me. I felt seen – I allowed myself be seen.

I was taken aback by my reaction to this visit. Had my stay here been bad? My eyes were opened in a way I had never thought possible.

I thought I'd remember how difficult my time in the NRH had been but the institution had no power over me anymore; in fact I felt a calmness here. It had a different vibe, a different feeling – a feeling of contentment and ease, gratitude and wonder.

As I was going up in the lift towards the second floor, I caught my reflection in the mirror. I'd previously refused to look in that mirror. The sickly, gaunt face I'd once had, was now replaced by a made-up face with black mascara and dusty-pink lipstick. My hair was longer and I was wearing jeans and a fitted white shirt. I'd proper footwear which snuggled over my AFO (orthotic). I was an average woman of my age, a woman who hadn't been dehumanised by years of pain. But most importantly, I had an inner glow of happiness. I was a survivor. I was Kim again.

Alighting from the lift, I took a quick peak into the room I had spent nearly two months in. It held no real affinity for me. Had I really slept in there? I moved on towards the men's section of St. Bridget's Ward. Automatic doors opened and I ventured in. It was much brighter than I'd remembered. I had only been in this ward in the early, dark, winter mornings when I was going to or from the shower, and in December and January the lights were always on. Back then I had struggled through the ward, either on foot or in a wheelchair. I had diverted my eyes during times of exposure and shame. Now I was smiling warmly at some of the male patients as I scanned the beds for my friend.

Even after my friend had been discharged, I revisited the NRH a few times. I would sit in the coffee shop on my own, watching and thinking. Being ensconced in this environment was helping me face one of the final stages of my grieving process: acceptance. I'd never accept the stroke as something good, but I recognised that it had happened and that it had happened to me. That acknowledgement helped me move forward towards happiness.

But I couldn't let go of the shame. *It's still my fault...*

It wasn't my fault

2012

I WAS becoming accustomed to attending The Mid-West Regional Hospital as an out-patient. The red 'full' sign over the car-park was nearly always lit and the number of smokers at the hospital entrance door hadn't reduced.

My appointment was for 10.30 a.m.

When I approached the secretary in the waiting area to let her know I'd arrived, I got 'the look' from other patients who were watching me inquisitively. This time I knew it wasn't due to my exaggerated limp or involuntary bent elbow and furled fingers. In situations when people are already seated, they tend to stare smugly at the new arrivals. It's hospital etiquette – ha, you don't know what you're doing, don't know where to sit. I'm already settled in and I'll watch you fumble and hope you get embarrassed.

I pretended to be unconcerned by the observers, but unfortunately I tripped over the strap of my bag, stumbled and landed on a chair beside an elderly man. It was farcical. I'd experienced this mortification before, in Croatia, when I'd forgotten to throw the anchor into the sea in front of the coffee-drinking observers onshore, who were sneering at sailors' fauxpas. Like on our holiday, I was fulfilling the need of the crowd. They were pleased by the entertainment.

I'll show you. You'll bow your heads in shame when something like this happens to you.

No one even gazed over at me. A new patient had arrived and was scanning the corridor for somewhere to sit. How thrilling! But my mind had gone elsewhere – I'd a lot to sort out.

'Kim Maguire, Kim please.'

It had only been a twenty-minute wait and I was nearly disappointed I'd been fooled into thinking I'd be waiting on the corridor for longer. I hadn't my thoughts together and was afraid I wouldn't have the guts to carry out my questioning.

The consultation room was an innocuous space. It was a shared room for many doctors to use, and the standard anatomy charts weren't specific to any particular discipline. I could have been there to see any consultant in the hospital, but I wasn't.

'Good morning, Kim, please take a seat.'

'Thanks.'

Dr Boers was a warm man and I liked seeing him once or twice a year. He was soft-spoken, engaging and most importantly, he listened. I sat across the table from him, playing with my fingers nervously. This appointment was different to the others. I was well into my recovery and I was ready to ask my neurologist some burning questions, which up to this point, I'd been afraid to ask.

He spoke first. 'How have you been?'

'Very good, thanks Doctor. It's amazing how things can change. I'm happy with my life. I'm able to spend afternoons with my son after I collect him from the crèche. I never thought life could be so good: I'm so grateful I survived. My little boy needs me and I need him. Whilst I never returned to teaching, I am working a few hours a week and I love my new job.'

He raised his eyebrows, impressed, so I went on, 'It's good to contribute to society once more.'

'That's good to hear. Are your energy levels up to it? Are you getting tired?'

I heard the genuine concern in his question.

'No, I'm good. If I'm tired, I go for a nap. Life is good again.'

'How's your son?'

'He's four now and is the most wonderful thing in my life. It's been great not having an au pair anymore and becoming an independent woman again. I can do most things on my own, except put my hair in a pony-tail. A man's version of a pony-tail isn't quite the same as a woman's.' I said, remembering Kieran's last novel attempt.

We smiled at this, and I guessed women's grooming was the last thing on Dr Boer's mind. I didn't think he'd be carrying out any research into one-handed hair accessories in the near future. Perhaps I should have said something more masculine like 'I can't bring in the coal or put bin-liners into the bins.' He must have seen the mischievous look in my eye and deftly moved the conversation forward.

'Any changes physically?' he said, lifting my left arm into the air.

305

'No I'm just the same. No changes in my arm or leg.'

It wasn't quite as difficult now, admitting the stark reality that my physical recovery had met its end. My hope of a 'miracle' cure had been put to rest. I was no longer looking at him in desperation. I had taken control of my disappointments by accepting the truth.

'How's the driving going?'

'Great. The independence is wonderful. I don't think I'd be doing so much if I hadn't the car. Both Kieran's and my car are automatic and are modified.'

Phew a good masculine answer!

'Well then I think we're finished, unless you have any questions?'

I breathed in and tried to control my racing heart. This was the time. This was when the truth could really knock my recovery back. I didn't know how I'd cope hearing answers I didn't want to hear. But it was time.

My main fear was that I'd hear the brain haemorrhage could have been prevented, meaning human error was to blame and if that were so, I didn't know how I'd forgive myself or the perpetrator.

I started, 'Do you think the fertility drugs over the years caused the brain haemorrhage?'

'No, those drugs would have been well out of your system. Kim, your CT scans imply you had an AVM.'

I looked at him and waited for him to explain what that meant.

'An AVM is an arteriovenous malformation. It's caused when an artery and a vein join together when they shouldn't. Everything points to you having a week blood vessel in your brain.'

'How did the malformation happen?'

It was time for me to hear about the bad life-style choices I'd made which had caused my stroke. Had my diet been to blame? Had my sweet tooth had an effect or perhaps I hadn't eaten enough vegetables? Had my compulsory reduction of exercise during the pregnancy caused it?

'An AVM is congenital: you're born with it. It was going to happen at some stage and you were unfortunate it happened so soon after your son was born, but at least he was born by then.'

'So if Dylan had been born a week later things could have gone very wrong? Kieran could have been left with neither wife nor child?'

'We'll never know.'

'Why me?'

'A small percentage of the population have AVMs which may go undiagnosed and may never rupture. Some people might get seizures, some might get headaches and many won't ever know they have an AVM and will go through life unaffected.'

'So it's not just me who had one. It's not just me whose body failed them?'

'No, others have AVMs too.'

'Was it caused by the C-section?'

'It's very unlikely.'

'Was it preventable?'

'No, you didn't even know you had it.'

'Did I not exercise enough?'

'No, that wasn't it.'

'Did I eat too much cake?'

'No.'

'Did I do something wrong?'

'No you didn't.'

'Was it my fault?'

'No.'

All that shame for no reason.

Epilogue

2014

THE last road sign we had passed said that Nicosia was only 12 km away. I was finding it hard to engage in the conversation which was going on between my son and husband about slides in a waterpark in Limassol.

'But Dad, Mummy said that slide was only for big persons, not for five-year-olds.'

'You can sit on my lap and we'll go down together. I think it will be brilliant!' Kieran replied.

'Mummy, it's your day today and it's my day tomorrow. Isn't that right?'

'Yes, your day tomorrow, pet.'

'Are you so excited about the waterpark?'

I didn't hear him.

'Mummy, I'm talking to you.'

'Yes, sorry. I can't wait for the waterpark,' I said, looking back at him.

All I could see was his red face as he sweated in a jumper he was refusing to take off, even in 28°C – fashion diva like his mother.

'It's your day today,' he repeated.

'Yes my day.'

It was my day. It was a huge day – one of the biggest days of my life. I was fulfilling a promise I had made to Kostas and Andry when I'd said goodbye to them at the door of the physiotherapy clinic some years before.

"I'll come back to see you in five years' time."

'Look Kim, there's IKEA,' Kieran said, pointing straight ahead.

I knew where we were. IKEA and The Mall of Cyprus were opposite Nicosia General Hospital. In a strange way I was more interested looking at the familiar shopping centre than at the hospital. The exterior of the hospital building held few memories for me – my memories were inside, in a ward.

'Only ten more minutes and we'll see Kostas and Andry,' I said, trembling in excitement.

My heart pumped faster than it had for a long time. I was coming home. I was meeting my saviours and I couldn't wait to see the physiotherapists who had given me back my legs. Few people in my life were as important as this selfless couple who had instilled confidence in me and had loved me unquestionably.

Kieran turned the car onto a narrow road and I recognised the building on my left – the old folks' home where I'd started my recovery. The sunshine disappeared as we descended into the basement car park.

Little had changed. A large generator was letting out little puffs of smoke to the right of us. Linen and disused mobility aids were still to the left of the entrance door. Everything was how it had been.

310

I got out of the car and could see Kostas approaching from the door of the clinic. His face lit up as he put his two arms around me.

'Keem, I'm so happy to see you!'

'And you Kostas.'

Our bodies were pressed against each other in an intimate way – a long-lost father-daughter reunion. I've never been embraced by someone for so long and when he eventually let me go, his eyes diverted to Kieran and Dylan who were standing behind us.

'Kieran, you are welcome,' he said, giving Kieran a big hug, even stronger than an ordinary 'man-hug'.

'Come, come. Andry is waiting for you.'

He stood back and let me walk in front of him. I knew he was analysing every muscle of mine which I was using to make me walk. He'd every right to.

We entered the clinic and I looked straight ahead down the corridor. Feelings of utter joy were flickering in and out of my chest. I had survived so much and I was now a different person, I was just an ordinary visitor now. Andry came out from behind a curtain where she was working with a patient.

'Kim, Kieran, Dylan!' she boomed, watching me walk towards her.

'Andry, it's so good to see you!'

It was my turn to initiate a huge embrace which was reciprocated in the same way it was offered. She looked me up and down.

'Wow! You doing very good.'

Kostas nodded in agreement.

They were the words I wanted to hear. My recovery was an endorsement of their work and I wanted them to be proud of themselves and proud of the work they had done.

I'd put in a lot of thought into how I'd present myself to them – what I'd wear and how I'd do my hair. A few years previously, my insightful friend, Jo, had once said; "the speed of your hair-growth is matching the rate of your growing strength."

My hair was now half way down my back.

Half my head had been shaved when they'd first met me and now I wanted them to see how I'd changed. But I should have remembered: they'd never been visually impaired – they'd always seen me under my illness.

We spent most of the afternoon with them, chatting over lunch. They wanted to know all that had happened when I'd left them and returned to Ireland.

It was magical being in their presence and I couldn't stop smiling. Our reunion was all I'd imagined it to be.

'We'd better go now,' Kieran said, when we'd eaten the huge mezze they had ordered for us in the restaurant.

We said goodbye and we drove towards Larnaca city.

The coastal route was the same one we'd taken the morning I'd gone into hospital to have Dylan.

'Slow down Kieran, I want to take it all in.'

'Do you remember going to that restaurant over there?'

'Yes, where I nearly lost Dylan.' I said, forgetting Dylan was in the car.

'Why? Where did I go?'

'Oh, I'm only joking. I wanted to see if you were listening,' I replied, tying to cover up my mistake. My five-year-old wasn't ready to hear I'd nearly miscarried him.

We arrived at the maternity hospital where I'd arranged to meet Dr Kassinis, the man who had brought Dylan into the world.

The hospital lobby and waiting area were smaller than I'd remembered. Kieran and Dylan went to find toilets and I sat anxiously outside of the consultation room.

Suddenly the door opened and a man with an enormous smile came over to me.

'Come, come.'

I went into the room. We looked at each other for a few seconds and I wondered if he remembered who I was.

'Keem, let me see you.'

He was grinning and nodding his head. He kissed me on both cheeks and I could feel the warmth of his face on mine.

'I 'ave 'ears in my eyes. I crying to see you.'

I looked at tears flowing down his chubby cheeks and it was only then it dawned on me that this visit meant a lot to him too. I had returned to see him again.

Kieran and Dylan came in and sat beside me.

'Hello Doctor,' Kieran said. 'We came back to Cyprus to meet you again. It's been five years.'

'I'm so happy to see you.'

Dr Kassinis looked at me and continued, 'You are a miracle. Keem, the Miracle!'

He was holding my hand tightly.

'Thank you,' I replied.

'You're lucky your husband act so fast and got you to hospital. I called the radiologist to come and when I saw the MRI scan, it didn't look good. I thought it wasn't good and I shook my head. But you are alive. I thought if you did lived, you be completely paralysed. You're a miracle! Your baby was the best thing to get you better and you also worked hard.'

I smiled at his words of disbelief. It was nice hearing I was a miracle and that my new-born baby and my determination had got me through the life-threatening situation.

'This little boy here made me live,' I said, smiling at Dylan as he started to get down off Kieran's lap and come over to me.

'Yes he did, he is very special. Would you like to see all of your pictures when you were in your Mummy's tummy?' Dr Kassinis asked Dylan, who was studying the 3D scan pictures on the computer screen.

Dr Kassinis looked up at me.

'It was very good to have the Caesarean section, otherwise it not good. Your blood vessels would have burst.'

His voice trailed as he pointed to his head and opened his fingers widely to make explosive signs.

His actions of demonstrating blood vessels rupturing, was further proof that the C-section didn't cause the brain haemorrhage. *Non coupable.* A natural birth would have killed me.

He re-engaged with Dylan and they started to laugh at Dylan's bottom which was evident to see in one of the pictures.

'You'd like some coffee?' he asked us.

'No, it's OK. We just came to say hello and to thank you for all you did for me,' I said, giving Kieran the eye that we should get on the road as it was now dark.

Dr Kassinis and Dylan posed for photos and then my former consultant put his arms around me and planted kisses all over my cheeks.

'You are a miracle. I so happy to see you. Thank you for coming. I'm very happy.'

And with that we left and drove back to our hotel in Pissouri, back where the pregnancy had started.

'I'm ecstatic! What a fantastic day!'

'Mummy, it's my day tomorrow.'

'Yes, your day tomorrow, my love.'

A chapter of my life closed.

THE END

Acknowledgements

FIRSTLY, I'd like to thank my husband Kieran and my little boy Dylan. My family; Dad, Mum, Carla, Ann, Philip, Peter, Rhian and nieces and nephews. My in-laws; Noel, Chris, Martin, Laura, Gary, Dermot, Fergal, Emer and David and spouses.

A sincere thank-you to my mentor David Rice, my editors, Fiona Clark-Echlin and Rosie Newcomb and everyone in my writers' group who encouraged me to write my story.

I am also indebted to the medical staff at UHG, UHL, NRH, St. Raphael's Hospital, Nicosia General Hospital. Dr Kassinis, Dr Ditis, Professor Michael Lee, Dr Boers, my G.P, physiotherapists; Kostas, Andres and Claire Noonan. The 16th and 17th Irish Contingents and the British Army Contingent. Maureen Gleeson and staff in The Derg Centre. All in ABI Ireland Limerick and North Tipperary Disability Services. Former work colleagues and friends in Cratloe. An Garda Síochána, The Garda Medical Aid, wonderful child-minders and all of the coffee-shops in Ballina - Killaloe, in which I wrote this book.

My sincere gratitude for the invaluable feedback I received from those of you who are in my book. You kindly gave me

316

permission to include you in my story and didn't object too much about the poetic licence I occasionally used.

I am grateful to my many friends who listened and supported my family and me and without whom, I would not have achieved as much as I did.

And to you my readers, thank you for reading my memoirs.

The Author

KIM MAGUIRE was born in in Glencullen in Co. Dublin. She went to teacher-training college in Limerick and graduated with a Master's degree in Education. She worked as a primary-school teacher for 17 years before her premature retirement in 2011. The picturesque village of Ballina-Killaloe on the River Shannon in Co. Tipperary is Kim's anchor, where she, her husband and son live.

'Who's Stroking my Baby? is Kim's first book and was written over a four-year period. She is constantly developing her writing skills under the direction of the renowned author, David Rice, at the Killaloe Hedge-School of Writing in Co. Tipperary.

Kim and Kieran at a Medal Ceremony in the UNPA during Kieran's tour of duty in Cyprus 2008

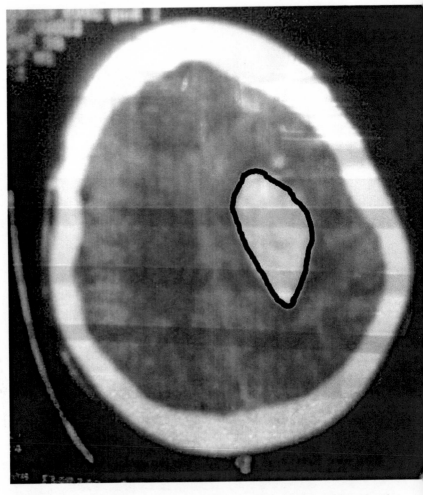

An MRI scan of Kim's brain taken on the night of her brain haemorrhage. The white area in the centre shows the extent of the bleed.

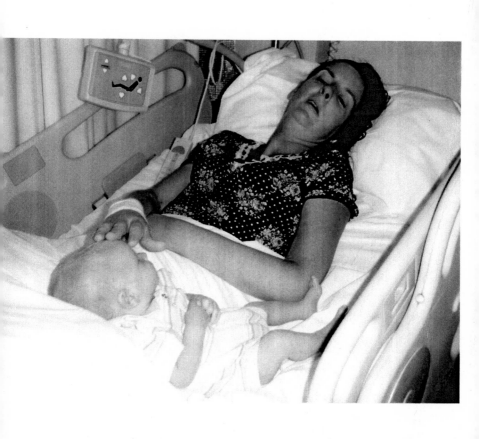

Dylan visiting his mother in hospital August 2009

**September 2009, Kim harnessed over a treadmill in the stroke
clinic with Kostas, the physiotherapist**

Kim with Dylan October 2009

Dylan's Christening - June 2010

Andry, Kim and Kostas, five years later in 2014